CORVETTE
50 YEARS

AMERICA'S FAVORITE SPORTS CAR

RANDY LEFFINGWELL
& TOM BENFORD

First published in 2003 by Motorbooks International, an imprint of MBI Publishing Company, Galtier Plaza, Suite 200, 380 Jackson Street, St. Paul, MN 55101-3885 USA

Material in this book was derived from *Corvette: 50 Years* by Randy Leffingwell, published by MBI Publishing Company in 2002.

© Tom Benford, 2003

All photography by Randy Leffingwell unless otherwise noted.

Motorbooks International titles are also available at discounts in bulk quantity for industrial or sales-promotional use. For details write to Special Sales Manager at Motorbooks International Wholesalers & Distributors, Galtier Plaza, Suite 200, 380 Jackson Street, St. Paul, MN 55101-3885 USA.

ISBN 0-7603-1768-2

Editor: Amy Glaser
Designer: Chris Fayers

Printed in China

Contents

IN THE BEGINNING . . .

CHAPTER ONE

IN THE BEGINNING . . .

General Motors was created with the objective of becoming an automotive giant, and it has been the world's largest company for many years. GM's master plan was to have an automaker for each niche, ideally taking customers from its entry-level Chevrolet models up to the luxury Cadillac line. The divisions were originally semi-autonomous, with different bodies and engines, but that was slowly eliminated over the years in the name of efficiency.

William Durant, the founder of GM, said a wallpaper pattern he saw in a Paris hotel in 1908 inspired the bowtie logo. Legend has it, he ripped off a small piece of the wallpaper and brought it back to Detroit. The bowtie logo was used for the first time in 1914.

In 1926, Lawrence P. Fisher, the general manager of Cadillac, discovered a talented 32-year-old designer named Harley Earl doing custom coachwork at a Cadillac dealership in Hollywood and hired him as a

Previous pages and this page: *Art Oberly at McCullough Supercharger Company in Venice, California, offered to develop his product to work on Corvette's Blue Flame Six to improve performance. General Motors agreed, but it had promised early production cars to VIPs. This one, #24, was meant for the president of Standard Oil Company. History is vague, but it seems the oil man got this car to Venice where Oberley and Erik Kaughman installed the first supercharger and gave the car its distinctive hood badge.*

By the time this car rolled out of the Flint plant, creative minds already were devising ways to make the sports car more sporty. While Chevrolet's Tom Keating and Ed Cole had been given the go-ahead to produce a Chevrolet V-8, few outside GM engineering knew it.

consultant. Earl designed the body for the 1927 LaSalle, the first edition of Cadillac's companion make. The car was a huge success. Earl was hired to work for the company full time, with the specific task of setting up an in-house styling department. Earl's Art and Colour Section was an industry first. (The British spelling of "colour" was Earl's way of denoting prestige.) In 1937, he renamed the department the Styling Section, to reflect a new focus on design.

The ever-innovative Harley Earl introduced two types of design methods to General Motors. One was two-dimensional rough sketches consisting of line drawings from different viewing perspectives, and the other was three-dimensional clay models, which were presented as realistic mock-ups for review and approval by management.

The United States was up to its chin in the Korean conflict in the early 1950s. Steel was crucial for manufacturing automobiles, but it was also essential for making the tanks, ships, and shells bound for Korea. The steel shortage caused by the war effort had automakers thinking about alternative materials.

Fiberglass was the most appealing alternative. By 1952, GM and the entire industry had known about this

Previous: *Molding the plastic body to "Sparky" Bohnstedt's bullet taillights caused fiberglass body makers terrible problems. Restorers now moan about the delicate multi-piece rear bumper assemblies. Airflow over the rear stalled exahust fumes, and early cars often discolored around the protruding pipes.*

Below: *Art Oberly and Erik Kaughman added twin vacuum-pressure gauges, mounting them on a production-looking bracket. Because of the length of tubing required to move the compressed supercharged air around the engine, one gauge monitors pressure out of the supercharger and the other checks it as it enters the carburetors.*

This was a car engineered in Harley Earl's styling department. Chevrolet's General Manager Tom Keating and others agreed it could greatly help Chevrolet regain its shrinking audience, so the car was hurried into production. Engineers took just enough time to change fanciful ideas into an automobile that could come off an assembly line and go around a corner. The 1953 and 1954 Corvettes represented a remarkable achievement.

McCullough's supercharger is visible at the right front corner of the engine compartment. A flexible hose links it to the three stock Carter carburettors connected by another solid red-painted tube dubbed the "log". Because the supercharger was

large, Oberly and Kaughman repositioned the factory air cleaner out of the engine compartment and into the upper rear of the right front fender, a kind of early "cold box" intake.

material—also called glass reinforced plastic (GRP)—for two decades. GM had some experience with fiberglass. During World War II, Cadillac scrapped the tooling for its body fenders. After the war ended, the company found that the fiberglass material was a quick way to make replacement fenders.

Southern California boat builders had been using the easily shaped material for years to produce low-maintenance hulls. Bill Tritt, a boat maker from near

Santa Barbara, started the Glasspar Company in 1950. He and his partners got a call from an air force major, Kenneth Brooks, who wanted to give his wife a Jeep for her personal use, but he wanted it to look better than a boxy Jeep. Tritt took the job and completed the car body made of fiberglass early in 1951. He named it the *Boxer*, but it quickly became known as the *Brooks Boxer*. It looked good, and its light green color attracted attention.

The only visible differences between a normal early production 1953 model and this supercharged car are the script badge on the nose and replacement of Chevrolet's steel wheels with 1953 Buick Skylark wire wheels. Otherwise, nothing gives away the

substantial improvement in performance offered by the McCullough blower. the nose and replacement of Chevrolet's steel wheels with 1953 Buick Skylark wire wheels.

A local sales engineer from U.S. Rubber was very interested in the car. The company's Naugatuck, Connecticut, chemical division produced Vibrin, a polyester plastic that Tritt had used as a key ingredient in the mix of his GRP. Naugatuck's Vibrin sales director, Dr. Earl Ebers, had tried unsuccessfully to get his product into a Detroit design studio, and he hoped the *Boxer* might be his key in. Glasspar and Naugatuck collaborated on making four more *Boxer* bodies in February 1952.

The U.S. Rubber Company's Naugatuck chemical division also had another compound. It was a cloth the company also wanted to see used in automobiles, called *Naugahyde*.

Sportsman Red, Polo White, and black exterior cars had red interiors.

Chevrolet engineering called Ebers, who acquired the *Brooks Boxer* and showed it at the National Plastics Exposition in mid-March 1952. He met other Chevy engineers during the show, and from their reactions, he decided to drive the car directly to GM's styling auditorium. Ebers and his staff showed engineers they could take a mold from a fender and make an exact duplicate out of fiberglass.

Chevrolet engineering and GM styling quickly adopted the material for experimental car bodies and dream cars. They also used it on prototype and show cars to replace conventional plaster of Paris-over-wood forms, which they previously would cover with hand-hammered steel.

There, in his own styling auditorium in March 1952, Harley Earl examined the fiberglass-body car in depth. He saw materials that were the next advance in his car design/model-making process, a substance that could be used to fabricate something in prototype form quickly and easily. He also saw before him a type of automobile that had been in his head for some time.

An American Sports Car

In the late 1940s, Harley Earl came up with the idea that America needed a sports car. He loved sports cars himself, and after World War II, returning GI's were bringing home exotic little two-seaters that were real performers. Italy had its Ferraris and Alfa Romeos. English car makers produced the sensuous Jaguar XK-120, the spindly MG-TC, Aston Martins, and Triumphs. These were primarily intended for export sale in North America, but they sold to so few Americans that the domestic makers paid little attention to them. But Harley Earl noticed.

For 1953, GM President Harlow Curtice approved a traveling series of product-preview shows to gauge the

Previous pages: *Briggs Weaver designed two identical roadsters and a coupe for Cunningham. They weighed 2,400 pounds, nearly 900 pounds less than Cunningham's previous models, and these new cars were slightly smaller as well.*

Above: *By the time the Corvette celebrated its 25th anniversary in 1978 the engine had lost some of its steam of pollution controls, but the Corvette still provided more excitement than most cars available at that time.*

Corvette again paced the Indy 500 but this time the color scheme was harder for many people to take. Wild graphics adorned a Pace Car Purple finish. The package included bright yellow-painted wheels though these magnesium wheels were a popular option. Chevrolet produced 1,163 replicas (for an extra $5,039) and most owners quickly removed the gaudy exterior graphics decals.

public's reactions to new body and model styles. He named the touring shows Motorama. That year, Earl introduced the Cadillac El Dorado and Le Mans; the Oldsmobile Fiesta, Wildfire, and Starfire; the Buick Skylark and Wildcat; and the Pontiac Parisienne. The Starfire, Wildfire, and Le Mans were fiberglass. The 1953 Motorama shows also featured a sporty two-seat roadster from Chevrolet.

For his sports car, Earl fit a stylish two-seat body around a production engine and frame. He wanted to use a V-8 engine, but since Chevrolet didn't have a V-8 at the time, he used the Chevrolet six-cylinder engine. Virtually every sports car of the period emulated the long hood/short rear deck style of the classic 1930s cars, and Earl followed that convention.

Near the end of spring, on June 2, 1952, Earl finally showed the finished full-size clay model to a small group. For this showing, Curtice brought along Chevrolet general manager Tom Keating and chief engineer Ed Cole. Cole and Keating were thrilled, Cole, by some accounts, almost jumping in excitement. This was the car they wanted for Motorama.

THE CORVETTE MAKES
ITS DEBUT

CHAPTER
TWO

chapter two

THE CORVETTE MAKES ITS DEBUT

1953–1955

The code name for General Motors' new sports-car program was Project Opel. Ed Cole ordered one car to be completed to show standards in time for the 1953 Motorama opening on January 17. Tom Keating and Harley Earl agreed to build the show car out of fiberglass; if it ever went into production, the plan was to fabricate it in steel.

Many forces were at work within GM to get the car ready by show time. Maurice Olley began engineering the hastily drawn chassis to meet GM's production procedures. At first he revised the 1949 sedan's front suspension to fit inside the slim body designed by Bob McLean, but ultimately, Olley had to design a new frame to accommodate the low, rearward placement of the engine. The new frame was formed of steel boxed-section side-members tied together with a central crossing X-member. Though this new frame was low enough to allow the drive-shaft to ride above it, it was an expensive design, so compromises elsewhere were necessary.

Earl and Cole conceded to use the in-line six-cylinder Chevrolet engine, and improving the performance of the standard "Blue Flame Six" was the prime objective of Cole's staff. Harry Barr, a colleague of Cole's on the development of the Cadillac V-8, joined him at Chevrolet. By adding mechanical lifters, an aluminum intake manifold straddled by three single-barrel Carter carburetors, dual exhausts, and increasing the compression

Previous pages and this page: Although the new factory in St. Louis had the capacity to produce 10,000 cars a year, Chevrolet produced just 3,640 Corvettes for 1954, fully a third of which remained unsold at the end of the year.

By midyear, Chevrolet had remedied the exhaust staining problem by fitting exhaust pipe extensions. These moved the gases out into the airstream coming over the rear of the car and out away from the body. These were stainless steel.

While Chevrolet introduced the Corvette at $3,733 fully equipped in 1953, it listed the base price at $3,498. For 1954, it reduced the base price to $2,774.

from 7.5:1 to 8.0:1, Barr coaxed 150 horsepower from the mill, an improvement of 35 horsepower over the stock motor. Rechristened the "Blue Flame Special," it still came up short against the Jaguar's 180 horsepower.

Earl and Cole wanted a manual gearbox for the new car, but no four-speed manual transmissions were available in the United States. Deferring to time and cost concerns, they decided to use the reliable two-speed Powerglide automatic transmission in the car. Another plus was that it mated perfectly to the engine that fit the Olley-McLean package.

Myron Scott, chief photographer for the Campbell-Ewald ad agency, came up with a name for the car. He admired the fast naval vessels that performed patrol duties during World War II as destroyer escorts in North Atlantic convoys. Scott suggested using the same name as these boats, Corvette, for the new car. Harley Earl liked it immediately.

Off and Running

The car debuted at the 1953 Motorama, its Polo White fiberglass finish glistening under the spotlights in the

Both 1953 and 1954 models operated on 6-volt electrical systems. Turn-signals were a $16.75 option, though like all 1953 and 1954 Corvette options, both cars were built with all the options included. Wide whitewall tires—6.70x15— were another standard option.

Waldorf Astoria Grand Ballroom. The Corvette name was displayed in simple script across the car's nose.

> ## The original front emblem and horn button on EX-122, the "Motorama" Corvette, featured crossed American and checkered flags. The company soon discovered that using an American flag on a product trademark was against the law. The emblem was changed before the Motorama debut.

The show car was enthusiastically received by the nearly 2 million people who attended the six-city Motorama tour. Bolstered by this warm response, GM management decided to start production before 1954. The search was on to find a company to manufacture the fiberglass body parts.

Robert Morrison was the president of the Molded Fiber Glass Company (MFG), a concern that produced molded glass-reinforced plastics products, including fiberglass bread palettes for Wonder Bread. He had previously contacted GM in the hopes of getting his company involved in manufacturing fiberglass parts for the auto industry.

On Monday, January 24, Morrison got a phone call from Chevrolet asking if some of their engineers could come to see the MFG plant the following day. Morrison agreed, and project engineer Carl Jakust and E. J. "Jim" Premo, the chief body engineer for the Chevrolet division, arrived on Tuesday.

The Chevrolet engineers took measurements of each fiberglass press. They planned to redesign their parts to fit Morrison's machinery. Morrison told them his presses were in use and that he'd buy new ones for the automobile project; he offered to help redesign the parts himself so that they not only would mold well but also would be strong.

Chevrolet had lost the youth market to postwar cars that had V-8 engines and convertible tops. They needed to get this two-seat sports car out as fast as possible, and

Below and opposite: *Chevrolet listed the automatic transmission, tires, and other previous standard equipment as options for 1954. This led some to believe that Chevrolet also offered a manual gearbox.*

the plan was to produce 50 each day. Despite skepticism within GM that MFG had the capacity to meet these production needs, MFG received a $4 million contract to produce fiberglass bodies for Chevrolet. Chevrolet wanted the first of the 300 complete sets of body panels before June 1.

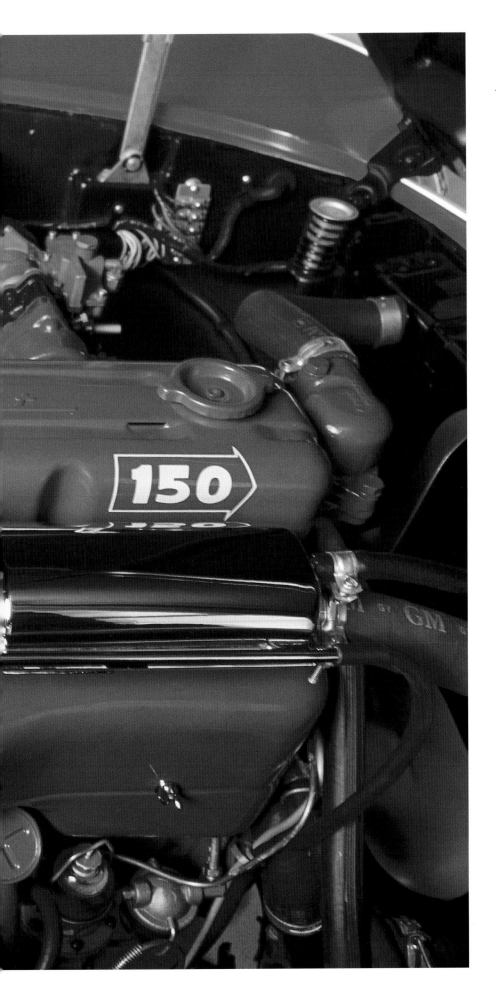

The Blue Flame Six persevered, still offering 150 horsepower (87 at the rear wheels) as it had through 1953. Sometime during the model year, Chevrolet revised camshaft lobes, increasing gross output to 155 horsepower. The Blue Flame and 150 decals were fitted only to painted valve covers. Some cars were delivered with chrome-plated covers, and these got no decals.

When MFG got the order, the entire fiberglass industry knew about it. Morrison only had four of his key people left after spinning off his tray-making operation. MFG, with the help of Owens-Corning, erected a new 167,000-square-foot building to construct the Corvette parts, but Morrison's organization was stretched thin. Chevrolet cooperated with manpower and resin suppliers, and Owens-Corning sent people in and paid their expenses. Competitors worked alongside each other to produce the parts. Chevrolet body engineers quickly learned from the suppliers the techniques for producing bodies.

One method was called hand lay-up. The engineering parts fabrication department at GM already used this slow, exact process to create Motorama Dream Cars and Earl's prototypes, including the Corvette. The "matched-metal die method" was similar to steel body production and offered many benefits. Large presses used either cast-iron or plate-steel molds that were mated to each other. Morrison's 15 new hydraulic presses compressed these molds together like steel-stamping dies to form the fiberglass panels under as much as 500 tons of pressure. In addition, matched-metal was the fastest process, and its molds offered the benefit of a production life of as many as 20,000 impressions.

Production of the car offered many challenges throughout the first year. The assembly plant in Flint, Michigan, was small, with a line long enough for only six chassis. Start-up was slow, grueling, and exhausting. It took work crews three 16-hour days to assemble the first car, which was completed on June 30. Through July, they were satisfied to finish one car a day. By August, three cars a day rolled off the line. Meanwhile, the line in St. Louis was being converted to become

With 195 horsepower now on tap and a three-speed manual transmission available to manage it, performance and driving excitement improved greatly.

Corvette's permanent home. On December 24, Chevrolet ended production at Flint and four days later production started in St. Louis.

> The first few dozen Corvettes were literally rolled off the assembly line, since they would not start. Electrical grounding to fiberglass bodies was a new experience for assembly-line personnel.

Taking It to the Streets

When the new Corvette hit the streets in September 1953, it landed more with a dull thud than a big splash. The price came in at $3,513, nearly twice Earl's target of $1,800. The Blue Flame Special engine and Powerglide transmission took the car from 0 to 60 miles per hour in 11 seconds and gave it a top speed of 105 miles per hour. By comparison, the Jaguar XK-120 cost $268 less, hit 60 miles per hour a second quicker, and went 25 miles per hour faster. The Corvette's side windows were sunlight-yellowing plastic, and the tops only came in black. Build quality was inconsistent. Assembly-line workers struggled to get machine-made bits to fit handmade bodies. The car suffered teething problems. It leaked water at the windshield and the top.

The first production Corvette (serial #E53F001001) came off the assembly line on June 30, 1953. Assembly-line worker Tony Kleiber had the honor of "driving" the first Corvette off the line. The Corvette was the first dream car to become a production model, and it was the first series-production car with a fiberglass body.

The Corvette was not a cheap car, but it sure acted like one. GM needed to rekindle the momentum that had been fading since the Motorama finale. Tom Keating was sensitive to public perceptions, and he attempted to put a positive spin on the car. In a statement released after the introduction, he said, "In the Corvette, we have built a sports car in the American tradition . . . to satisfy the American public's conception of beauty, comfort, convenience plus performance."

Chevrolet held a press introduction on September 29. Fifty journalists shared eight cars, and each drove a seven-mile course at GM's Milford Proving Ground. The Flint factory delivered a few more cars before October 1. Another 50 cars were offered through its highest volume dealers to an "A list" of handpicked, highly visible entertainers, prominent athletes, and executives from other major companies.

While Chevrolet directed its exclusivity toward the country-club set, the car was too crude for that market. On the other hand, sports car enthusiasts cried for more power and a transmission they could shift themselves.

Zora Arkus-Duntov

In May 1953, a month before Corvette production began, Chevrolet hired an ambitious, inventive engineer who first saw the Corvette as one of the crowd visiting New York's Motorama show. Zora Arkus-Duntov came in with good credentials. He and his brother Yura had earned respect as creative development engineers for camshaft designs and the Ar-Dun cylinder heads they had developed. Arkus-Duntov loved cars and had considerable racing and engineering experience throughout Europe. He helped several owners tame the handling of their early V-8-powered Allards. At the age of 44, he joined Ed Cole's staff and went straight to work for Maurice Olley.

Arkus-Duntov got into the first engineering Corvette as soon as he could. Pressing it to its limit, he found it to be a car in which the two ends were fighting each other. While the rear end's canted springs achieved Olley's goal of inducing understeer, the front end (made from modified sedan parts) caused oversteer, from which it was difficult to recover. It was too late to help the 1953 production cars. Still, Arkus-Duntov performed the first of countless mechanical surgeries he would undertake over the next 22 years.

Racer Briggs Cunningham had ordered a Corvette during the New York Motorama show, but when he got his he kept it only a week, judging it "not much of a car."

This was a car engineered in Harley Earl's styling department. Chevrolet's General Manager Tom Keating and others agreed it could greatly help Chevrolet regain its shrinking audience, so the car was hurried into production. Engineers took just enough time to change fanciful ideas into an automobile that could come off an assembly line and go around a corner. The 1953 and 1954 Corvettes represented a remarkable achievement.

The first 5 production Corvettes came off the assembly line devoid of outer driver-side rearview mirrors. The first 24 cars were delivered without full wheel covers and had only the small center caps found on Chevrolet passenger cars.

As a division, Chevrolet sold 1,342,480 cars in 1953; only 183 of them were Corvettes. The 306,000 Motorama visitors in New York who spoke unknowingly into the styling department's concealed microphones said they'd buy it if GM would build it. Some 20,000 people went to their local dealers hoping to order Corvettes they never had any chance of getting.

Sales improved in 1954, aided by the launch of a major advertising campaign. By June, the first magazine reviews appeared and production was up to 50 cars per day.

The engineering department made a few improvements to the 1954 model. They modified the camshaft, boosting horsepower to 155 horsepower. Chevrolet added two paint colors, black and Sportsman Red, all with red interiors. Late in the year, Corvettes began to appear in Pennant Blue with beige interiors. The black convertible top of 1953 was changed to tan for 1954.

Although the St. Louis plant had the capacity to produce 10,000 Corvettes a year, it manufactured just 3,640, and only 2,780 of them were sold. After 1953 and 1954 sales, Chevrolet found itself with a surplus of nearly 1,100 unsold cars on January 1, 1955.

The Corvette's first attempt at international racing came in 1954. A. F. Young entered one in the third annual 12 Hours of Sebring on March 7, to be co-driven by Jack Morton. Before the race began, however, Young withdrew the car.

As management wrestled with the Corvette's future, Clare MacKichan's Chevrolet studio and Ed Cole's engineers pressed ahead with revisions and updates. Styling wanted to use an egg-crate grille similar to that on the 1955 Bel Air, and it proposed a functional hood air scoop and several dummy louvers along the body panel behind the front wheels. They also wanted to rid the rear end of its troublesome taillight bullets. But there was no money. Colors could be changed for 1955—styling replaced Pennant Blue with Harvest Gold, and Sportsman Red became Gypsy Red—but they could barely touch the body.

Throughout 1954, the car still suffered from what reviewers and enthusiasts alike thought was insufficient

Above: *Most production V-8 1955 models came with the automatic transmission, now improved to near perfection. Historians estimate perhaps only 75 cars appeared with the 3-speed manual. Even fewer were delivered with speedometers reading in kilometers, not miles. Export Corvettes sported few other modifications.*

Previous: *While some 1954 engines appeared with blue enamel–painted valve covers, fitted with decals reading Blue Flame and 150, others left the St. Louis factory with chrome-plated covers, as this engine shows. Earlier production 1954 models carried over the three individual air cleaners Chevrolet used on the 1953 models, but later 1954 cars breathed through larger dual basket-type cleaners, reportedly used to decrease risk of engine compartment fire.*

Following pages: *Of the 700 cars manufactured, production records are scarce. Historians guess that about 325 of these were Polo White, 180 were Gypsy Red, another 120 were Harvest Gold, and just 45 appeared in this Pennant Blue. The rarest color seems to be Corvette Copper, with perhaps only 15 manufactured.*

horsepower. The engineering staff began developing a new 231-ci displacement V-8 overhead-valve engine. Ed Cole wanted to increase it to 265-ci displacement, and Tom Keating agreed. With Keating's endorsement, GM chairman Alfred Sloan approved the project without ever seeing plans. Now Cole needed engineers, and he hired hundreds, taking his staff up to 2,900 people. He believed the need for this engine was urgent. His staff designed it and built a running model in 15 weeks. Cole was so certain of the design that he ordered tooling and plant space before Barr and his engineers even fired up the 265 for the first time.

Cole's engineers were anxious to see how the new engine would affect the Corvette's performance, so they refitted the 1953 Motorama show car, EX-122, with a prototype V-8. It ran flawlessly for 25,000 miles out at Milford. Keating and Cole decided to offer it with a three-speed manual gearbox, in addition to the Powerglide, for 1955.

The new engine pumped life into the ailing Corvette. Performance jumped as 0–60 miles per hour times dropped three full seconds to eight in the late 1955 cars fitted with the three-speed. Top speed climbed to 120 miles per hour, and fuel economy improved from 17 to 20 miles per gallon.

The rejuvenated Corvette did not come a moment too soon for Chevrolet. In March 1954, Ford announced its own 160-horsepower, Y-block, V-8-engined Thunderbird with roll-up windows, to sell for $2,695. Production was to begin in September.

By the end of 1955, Ford sold 16,155 T-birds. Chevrolet had halted Corvette production midyear, stopping after assembling 700 cars. Chevrolet sold just 675, a few dozen of which were fitted with the manual gearbox.

These numbers would have sent ordinary men to the showers, defeated and humiliated. Earl, Cole, Keating, and Curtice were not ordinary men. Chairman Alfred Sloan had already said, "The question is not simply one of maximizing the rate of return for a specific short period of time . . . [but] the fundamental consideration was an average return over a long period of time." With the sales figures his other cars produced, he told his board it could

Physically, the 1955 model was identical to the previous two years although a new badge identified the optional V-8 engine. The "base" six-cylinder roadster held its price at $2,774, while the V-8 roadster started at $2,909 before the mandatory "options" were totaled in.

afford to be patient. Chevrolet research reported that 17 percent of American households were two-car families. Chevrolet once again outsold Ford overall in 1955, 1,646,681 cars to 1,573,276. Yet Ford had found 16,155 buyers where Chevrolet had not.

Chevrolet knew it had a home run with its V-8. The Corvette just had not yet caught the buyers' imaginations. Seeing the Thunderbird's success across town, Sloan further believed that the Corvette was the right car for GM and Chevrolet at the time, even if they didn't have the car "right" yet. Yet.

On October 15, 1954, Zora Arkus-Duntov wrote a memo to Ed Cole and Maurice Olley, noting that the Corvette appeared to be a failure. He suggested that to drop the Corvette, however, would be an admission of failure and a public embarrassment to all of Chevrolet. He suggested some modifications to the car and improvements to the sales effort. He wanted to create a separate department within Chevrolet to oversee Corvette development.

THE CORVETTE BECOMES
A CONTENDER

CHAPTER THREE

THE CORVETTE BECOMES A CONTENDER 1956–1958

By the time Tom Keating approved production of the Corvette for two more years, designers and engineers had little time to make substantial changes to entice buyers for 1956. Still, when the Motorama staff unveiled that year's Corvette at the Waldorf, it was clear that Earl's stylists and Cole's engineers had transformed the car.

In mid-December 1953, Zora Arkus-Duntov had written a memo that served as a wake-up call to the Chevrolet division at GM. He saw car-enthusiast magazines filled with stories about Ford. He believed Chevrolet could penetrate this market, and he proposed that they produce engine and chassis performance parts to market to the public.

Previous Pages: *It was supposed to look like the 1958 and 1959 models with four headlights and three front air intakes. Styling and engineering were nearly overwhelmed with big changes to the passenger car and pickup truck line, and they got swamped. Compounded by poor revenues from dismal 1954 sales, little time and no money meant only minor changes were possible for 1957.*

Opposite: *The introduction of Corvette's Regular Production Option (RPO) dual four-barrel carburetor, RPO 469, provided big news for 1956. Buyers felt the improvement from 195 to 225 horsepower. These six SR models, using RPO 449 with slightly higher-lift camshafts (the so-called Duntov cams), boasted 240 horsepower. SR models featured a shorter steering column to allow drivers more room to move their arms while cornering.*

"If the speed parts are carried as R.P.O. [regular production option] items for the Corvette," Arkus-Duntov wrote, "they will be recognized by the hot-rodders as the very parts they were looking for to hop up the Chevy." He saw that sports car enthusiasts inevitably will want to race the Corvette, and to do so they will put in a Cadillac V-8 engine to get more power. "I think this is not good!" he continued "Most likely they will meet with trouble—that is, breaking, sooner or later, mostly sooner, everything between flywheel and road wheels. Since we cannot prevent people from racing Corvettes, maybe it is better to help them do a good job at it." Arkus-Duntov believed that creating a sense of loyalty in Chevrolet buyers required faith that Chevrolet would produce what buyers wanted.

Duntov's work taming the handling of the 1956 production model established his chassis credentials within Chevrolet. The mark of Zora began to carry weight on his adopted car.

For the 1956 model Corvette, the Mercedes-Benz SL had replaced the Jaguar XK-120 as the main source of inspiration. When stylist Bob Cadaret finished the front of the 1956 Corvette, it resembled the 1954 SL. (Stylists commonly plagiarized each other. Jaguar's designers admitted duplicating a 1940 BMW race car for their XK-120.)

The new design also incorporated elements from Cadillac's 1955 Motorama LaSalle II dream car. The LaSalle II included a long, horizontal scallop in the body side. This feature now graced the Corvette, imparting a classic elegance to the side view and adding visual appeal while breaking up the panel. Cadaret also scalloped the taillights into the fenders. He achieved an economy of line by removing the excesses. The Corvette got roll-up

Following successful speed record attempts on Daytona Beach in February, Ed Cole committed Chevrolet engineers to a four-car effort for the 12 Hours of Sebring in March 1956. John Fitch supervised the effort, run from a hangar at the airport circuit. For five weeks, from February 18 to race day March 26, engineers worked in Florida and in Michigan to prepare parts for the cars.

All four of the racers received 37-gallon fuel tanks, limited slip differentials, Halibrand magnesium hubs, and knock-off wheels with Firestone Supersport 170 tires. Brakes were a challenge for racing. Fitch and Arkus-Duntov tried four systems before settling on Bendix Cerametallix linings inside Chevrolet's heavily finned cast-iron drums.

windows (with optional power windows available), outside door handles, and an optional power system for the convertible top.

The car came closer to realizing Arkus-Duntov's handling goals because the new 265-ci V-8 weighed 41 pounds less than the old Blue Flame Special. The V-8 was shorter and lower, which also helped handling. The engine, with its single Carter four-barrel carburetor, produced 210 horsepower; an optional second four-barrel raised output to 225 horsepower.

Speed compared to other cars caught people's attention. The Jaguar XK-120 in hottest trim reached 130 miles per hour; the Mercedes coupe was capable of 146 miles per hour. What if engineers could coax 150 miles per hour out of the Corvette on Daytona Beach speed runs?

Cole gave Arkus-Duntov clearance, and Arkus-Duntov moved to GM's Phoenix test track to determine how he could reach this speed. He needed another 30 horsepower, and engineering cast several wild cams from his designs to make this possible. Arkus-Duntov could now run the engine to 6,300 rpm, producing enough power to reach, theoretically, 163 miles per hour.

Chevrolet had given enthusiasts a sports car to race. Now they wanted to know what they should do to make it win.

In addition to Arkus-Duntov's road-racing experience, Cole had Mauri Rose on his staff. Rose was a three-time Indianapolis 500 winner who was working as a coordinator with private and dealer teams racing in NASCAR. Cole brought Rose and Arkus-Duntov to the Milford Proving Grounds in December 1955 to discuss racing Corvettes internationally. Frank Burrell, the engineer who had aided Briggs Cunningham's Cadillacs at Le Mans, was brought in to prepare the cars for the Sebring race in March, now barely 100 days away.

Cole quickly committed his two 1956 engineering department development cars plus a third preproduction model to the Sebring event. One car was already committed to Arkus-Duntov for the Daytona Beach Flying and Standing Mile speed records. After the Daytona runs, Burrell would get Arkus-Duntov's Corvette at a rented garage in Sebring to supervise its conversion to a road-racing car.

It took Arkus-Duntov until early January to get a certified two-way run averaging 150.58 miles per hour. He met his goal using an engine that produced 240 horsepower from parts soon to be available over the counter.

The crew went back to the official Daytona Speed Weeks in February with three cars, each engine with modified heads producing a 10.3:1 compression ratio and developing 255 horsepower. John Fitch, Arkus-Duntov, and Betty Skelton, a veteran automobile and airplane racer, each had a car to run.

Ford showed up with its Thunderbirds, and competition was fierce. Officials measured times not only for top speed runs but also for standing-start mile runs. At the end of the week, suffering from traction problems, John Fitch finished third (at 86.87 miles per hour) behind two Thunderbirds in the standing-start mile runs. In the flying mile, Arkus-Duntov averaged 147.3 miles per hour, beating all challengers.

To compete in production classes at Sebring, the Federation Internationale de l'Automobile (FIA), Sebring's race-sanctioning body, required that all race-car modifications had to be available to consumers. Manufacturers also needed to build at least 25 identical models for the racing version of the car to be classified as "production."

In response, Corvette created a new model for racing, the SR. Whether the initials meant "special racing" or "Sebring racer" remains uncertain. Engineering planned to equip the SR models with the Duntov camshaft, a semi-locked differential, a 37-gallon fuel tank, seat belts, Auburn clutch, Halibrand disc brakes, and quick-change wheels.

By late January, Fitch and Burrell were in Sebring working on the team, with a fourth car added by Fitch

CHAPTER THREE

Previous pages: *Stylist Dave Wheeler created the shapes that became famous not with Jerry Earl at the wheel but with dentist Dr. Dick Thompson. Dubbed the SR-2, the car proved too much of a handful for the younger Earl at its debut at Road America's June Sprints in 1956. Thompson took over. He found it too slow and heavy to be seriously competitive.*

Above: *Harley Earl loved European sports cars. Still, it annoyed him when his son Jerry purchased a Ferrari to go racing in SCCA events. Harley brought in a Sebring racer chassis and set his stylists to work building his son a better Corvette. Unfortunately, Harley's stylistic improvements to a pure production Corvette made it "modified" in SCCA's view, placing it against much tougher competition.*

after Daytona. Halibrand's disc brakes were not ready. Fitch knew Sebring was hard on brakes, so he and Burrell settled on newly designed large drums. Burrell cut cooling ducts into the drum backing plates, fed by large air vents ducted from the front grille through inner fender wells. He also had to modify the Carter carburetors; these sloshed fuel in hard cornering, flooding the engine and slowing the car. Cole's engineers had studied the Mercedes 300SL. Fuel injection was something they wanted to bring to the Corvette. The Sebring carburetor tests strengthened their resolve.

Burrell and Fitch got one V-8 bored out to 307 cubic inches and fitted it with a prototype Rochester fuel injection and a four-speed ZF gearbox from Germany. The increased displacement shifted it to B-class while the other three Corvettes remained in class C.

Sixty cars started the Sebring race and, typically, 24 finished. Two of the Corvettes quit early. Class C car #5 quit after an hour, victimized by a broken rear axle. A second car from Class C, #7, retired with a burned piston after two hours. The #6 car finished 15th overall, running with only top gear for hours. A virtually dealership-stock entry, #3, finished next to last. Fitch's B-class car, #1, worried him when its clutch began failing by the second lap, but his Le Mans experience had taught him how to nurse ailing race cars. He brought the car in ninth overall, first in Class B. For anyone who knew racing, it was an impressive debut. The cars won respect from their competitors and the crowd.

Cole and company analyzed the problems. Brakes plagued them at Sebring. Production brakes were inadequate

The "Fuelie" Is Born

One of the first projects completed in GM's new Engineering Center in suburban Warren, Michigan, was one that had been initiated in their former home in an old, drafty bank building downtown. Intent on improving intake/exhaust flow on the 265, engineering increased cylinder bore, yielding a 283-ci engine. For 1957, Corvette offered two four-barrel carburetors with the engine, to produce 245 horsepower. A still-hotter version cranked out 270 horsepower. The wildest tune developed 283 horsepower, the first GM engine to make one-horsepower-per-cubic-inch-of-displacement. It did it with Ramjet Fuel Injection, Chevrolet's production successor to the Rochester experimental system (which Burrell had run on Fitch's 1956 Sebring B-class winner). Of the 6,338 Corvettes produced for 1957, 1,040 had the "Fuelie" Ramjet injection.

for even the six-cylinder engines with automatic transmissions. For competition with a 255-horsepower V-8, the only combination that was proven to stay the distance was Bendix Cerametallix linings inside heavily finned iron drums, but they were heavy, making the Corvette heavier, too.

The selection of brakes was a decision that had ramifications far beyond race day. It established ethics for future considerations of balancing reduced weight against enhanced safety, comfort, or performance. Zora Arkus-Duntov said these brakes represented "a watershed decision that took the Corvette irrevocably in the direction of a larger, heavier car, barring any possible return to a lightweight design concept."

Before 1956 ended, Ed Cole succeeded Tom Keating as Chevrolet division general manager. Chevrolet had produced only 3,467 Corvettes, while Ford sold more than 15,000 of its Thunderbirds. Chase Morsey, a Ford product planner, set the Thunderbird's direction, and design chief

Frank Hershey concurred with Morsey's vision. Ford Thunderbird was to be a personal car, something that buyers knew fit between a sports car and a family passenger car. Chevrolet, they concluded, could keep trying with its poorly selling sports car.

The End of (Official) Corporate Racing

Alfred Sloan's intention had been to restyle car bodies every other year. Ed Cole knew Chrysler and Ford had new bodies on much of their 1957 lineups, but engineering delays held up GM's introductions. The car had too many new elements, and the studio couldn't handle it: a new engine, gearbox, chassis, suspension, body, and interior. Due to limited time and dismal production and sales of 1954, a quick nip and tuck was all that was possible for the 1957 Corvette model year.

Stylist Robert Cumberford, from Chuck Jordan's Studio 5, and Tony Lapine, from drafting, were assigned to work on the intended 1957 Corvette. They were given a windowless 20- by 40-foot room, which had been Harley Earl's temporary office before a permanent one was completed. Every studio in the building had a name or a number. Cumberford had a photostat made of an X and put it up on the door of their room, christening it "Studio X."

Only 664 of the 6,338 cars Chevrolet delivered in 1957 were fitted with the four-speed gearbox. *Road & Track* recorded 0–60 miles per hour times of 5.7 seconds in a test car with a 4.11:1 rear axle.

Harley Earl had ways of getting the most from his designers. He rarely dictated and never gave clear, precise instruction. He purposely kept his suggestions vague, and by changing direction often and unexpectedly, Earl gave his designers the greatest possible latitude to use their imaginations.

"We had no direction from anybody," Cumberford recalled. "Zora would come in, and he and Tony would tell stories." Lapine raced in Europe, as had Arkus-Duntov, and Cumberford had designed race cars in California before taking his job at GM. The three of them shared this interest. So some tasks, especially those that were racing related, just walked in the door. The SR-2 project was one of them.

A car was brought into the studio in early May, the body was taken off, and molds made. The windshield panel was the same as on the Sebring car. There was no headrest on it at the beginning, and the fin was added later as well. Other than extending the front out 10 inches to make a better aerodynamic line over the hood, there were very few changes. Basically, it was a stock Corvette, right down to the radio.

Arkus-Duntov took the car to the styling mechanical assembly shops, where he supervised SR-type modifications. At the June Sprints at Elkhart Lake, Wisconsin, Jerry Earl, Harley's son, entered the car, the first SR-2, but national-championship contender Dick Thompson drove it. To the Sports Car Club of America (SCCA), however, the stylized bodywork made the racer a "modified" car. At the end of its race against much leaner machines, Thompson said the car needed a lot of weight removed. When it came back to Detroit, the mechanical shops removed about 300 pounds from the SR-2 without doing anything obvious.

Before long, though, Earl was pursuing new interests. Dissatisfied with the half-effort of the SR-2, he wanted a full-on styling exercise to go racing. Earl acquired a white D-type Jaguar and proclaimed, "Let's use the D-type, change the body, and drop a Chevy into it. And let's go to Sebring and beat everybody!" Earl and his main supporter for the plan, heir-apparent Bill Mitchell, outlined their intentions to Ed Cole and Harry Barr, the Chevrolet division's chief engineer. Soon thereafter work started on a car that would become the SS Corvette.

Zora Arkus-Duntov purchased a Mercedes 300SL, and they took the body off to reveal its tubular space frame. Once the body was off the 300SL chassis, Arkus-Duntov put the chassis up on steel stands. He then put a Chevrolet engine, transmission, and differential beside it. He made a tube frame out of wooden dowels, copying the Mercedes around Chevrolet running gear.

They couldn't get a Corvette engine to fit the space of the Jaguar engine in the D-type without some major modifications, and Arkus-Duntov didn't want to do that. He wanted his own car, as did Harley Earl, and the result was the SS.

Internally, the car was referred to as the XP-64, the letters standing for Experimental Pursuit. Ed Cole funded one car. Arkus-Duntov, through creative accounting methods, got enough spare pieces fabricated to assemble a second car, a vehicle dubbed "the mule." They built this test car, partially skinned in rough fiberglass, to evaluate innovations in the XP-64. The mule's engine developed much less horsepower than the aluminum-head 283-ci V-8 with special fuel injection that Harry Barr's engineers were preparing.

Arkus-Duntov and his engineers had developed a remarkable braking system. In competition, Arkus-Duntov learned that the rear brake lines were too small. This caused a delay in system response that delivered spectacular brake lockups at the worst possible moment. Arkus-Duntov eventually used larger diameter tubing.

In Friday practice at Sebring, both Juan Manuel Fangio, the Argentine grand prix world champion, and English racer Stirling Moss drove the mule, turning exceptionally fast times. Chevrolet had contracted with Fangio to drive the race, but the actual car arrived late, missing Fangio's cutoff date. This released him to drive a Maserati, with whom Moss also had a contract. So John Fitch, who

This was Corvette's first Sebring class winner, driven by Dr. Dick Thompson and Swiss racer Gaston Andre. At the end of 12 hours, they had finished 12th overall, 1st in GT class. This car and its victory codified Arkus-Duntov's idea to make high performance parts available through dealers. Many racers benefited from the competitive advantages of RPO 684, a complete suspension package that also included brake ventilation.

was managing Sebring production Corvette efforts, stepped in. He contacted Italian grand prix and endurance champion Piero Taruffi, who flew overnight from Rome to join him.

They qualified the mule on the front row. Race morning revealed the magnesium-bodied car in its Harley Earl–specified blue finish. It was completed to spectacular Motorama show standards, but it suffered problems of inconsistent brake balance and hellish cockpit heat. The magnesium panels trapped the heat that the fiberglass insulated from the drivers. Tin snips slashed the sleek body.

Fitch started the race. As he had done the year before nursing a failing clutch, he quickly found a rhythm that kept the brakes from locking while cutting lap times to within a second of Fangio's qualifying effort. Yet problems and failures continued.

Taruffi noticed that the car's handling was deteriorating badly. The rear tires bounced into the body or hopped frantically after each bump in the concrete surface. Overheated himself, Taruffi pulled in and engineers found the car was undrivable after only 23 laps.

Despite the Sebring result, Ed Cole still saw a future in racing the SS and continuing Corvette promotion. Arkus-Duntov had given him a ride in the mule, and Cole promptly approved manufacture of three more cars to race at Le Mans, France. He let Arkus-Duntov begin work on a valve gear without springs for the top end of the engine. This could permit 400 horsepower at 9,000 rpm. Cole authorized construction of a 1958 model and making improved SR-2 models available to private entries.

When a Mercedez-Benz entry crashed horrifically during the 24-hour race at Le Mans in June 1955, the tragedy moved accountability onto every company president's agenda. Mercedes withdrew from racing that day; unfavorable publicity shadowed the company for years. No American automaker would risk the kind of public outcry or government scrutiny such an incident might inspire.

General Motors chairman Harlow Curtice suggested to the Automobile Manufacturers Association (AMA) during its February 1957 board meeting that member companies "take no part in automobile racing or other competitive events involving tests of speed, and that they refrain from suggesting speed in passenger car advertising or publicity." Every member ratified Curtice's proposal.

Factory participation in racing never stopped, however; it just learned to hide better. In fact, Chevrolet delivered 51 Corvettes in 1957 and 144 in 1958 manufactured with RPO 684. This provided heavy-duty front and rear springs and shock absorbers, metallic brake linings, and heavily finned brake drums as well as fresh air ducting to rear brakes and air scoops to cool the front brakes. These last two were nicknamed "elephant ears and trunks."

As racing took a backseat in the wake of the AMA proclamation, other designs were already in the works at GM for what would become the 1958 Corvette. One was strongly influenced by the 1956 Motorama Oldsmobile Golden Rocket with the Torpedo top. According to Robert Cumberford, this car was probably the true source of the split-window Corvette of 1963.

For the 1958 model, Cumberford wanted a car on a 94.5-inch wheelbase, an aluminum body and frame, an aluminum V-8 in front, and a full transaxle at the back. A more radical proposal came from Chevrolet engineering, which was developing a rear-mounted transmission and differential with the starter incorporated in the casing, designated "Project Q." It incorporated a full independent suspension that would have gone into production for the 1960 model year Chevrolet sedans. No one could justify it solely for a sports car that sold less than 6,400 units in 1957, but Corvette could easily adopt it from a passenger car line selling hundreds of thousands.

The full-size clay models and their accompanying engineering proposals for the 1958 car took the Corvette far beyond what the production 1958 model would be. Design and engineering made it equal to the most advanced, sophisticated sports—and racing—cars built anywhere in the world.

This was RPO 579E, Corvette's 283-ci engine with 283-horsepower output through Chevrolet's new Rochester fuel injection. It had long been a GM Engineering goal to develop one horsepower for each cubic inch of displacement. Output of this racing version was closer to 305 horsepower. It was good enough to give the car a 20-lap victory at Sebring over the nearest Mercedes-Benz 300SL.

Headed in the Wrong Direction

The 1958 introduction had progressed to full-size clay models but was soon scrapped. Instead, the production studio did a quick facelift on the 1956 to have it ready for production by fall 1957. Overall length grew from 168 to 177.2 inches. The car swelled 2.3 inches in width to 72.8. For sports car enthusiasts, the Corvette was headed in the wrong direction.

It was, however, a better automobile. Bumpers secured to the frame provided true accident protection. Acrylic lacquer replaced the nitrocellulose paints. Every instrument on the dash, except the clock, was relocated in front of the driver's eyes, with a large 160-miles-per-hour speedo surrounding the 6,000-rpm tachometer. Improvements under the hood made up for added girth. Output reached 290 horsepower with the Rochester fuel injection.

The new model year was introduced half a year after General Motors' official adoption of the AMA racing ban. GM could not and would not promote racing or speed. If a customer wanted to order certain things, however, all he needed to do was read the order form. Chevrolet would never argue with its customers. One customer, Jim Jeffords, filled out the order form at a Chicago dealership and found everything necessary except the car's exterior color. Inspired by a popular song, Jeffords painted the car a bright purple and named it *The Purple People Eater*. He won the SCCA B-production championship, and under the full force of the auto industry's prohibition, Chevrolet's own carefully created RPOs heralded the birth of the muscle car in America.

THE STRETCH

CHAPTER FOUR

chapter four

THE STRETCH

1959–1962

The seven-year stretch from 1956 to late 1962 meant different things to different people. To customers watching the Corvette in dealer showrooms, the car moved forward in appearance slightly, following fashion as it shed fins and gathered double headlights, but it got much better mechanically, gaining muscle and agility. Behind the scenes, for Cole's engineers and Earl's stylists, it was a time of walking, running, and sometimes sprinting on a treadmill. Lots of work got done, but few people outside the studios ever saw it or knew of it until years later.

William L. Mitchell inherited Harley Earl's job as vice president of styling at GM on December 1, 1958, when he was 46. He had worked for Earl for 22 years, starting as a stylist. Mitchell loved automobiles. He had worked as an illustrator for the publishing and road-racing Collier family and filled his office with his own drawings of classics. The Colliers owned these kinds of cars, and they invited Mitchell into their close-knit circle of enthusiasts, where he made rapid stylized sketches of them racing. Earl saw these and hired Mitchell in 1935.

Mitchell watched his mentor work. He knew Earl had had to prove himself and the value of styling to skeptical division general managers. Now he had to fight his own battles against other successors who seized the opportunity of Earl's departure to try to regain control. Some in GM management wanted to curtail styling's flamboyance

Previous Pages and Opposite: Normally cars painted Inca Silver appeared with white coves, though frequently second or third owners have eliminated the contrasting colors to unify the appearance, as Leonard Nagel has done with his 1959 convertible. All the colors received new names if not new formulation for the new model year.

CALIFORNIA
19 ⊙ 59
56
RAV 685

Chevrolet offered two fuel-injected versions of its 283-ci engine: the RPO 579 that provided 250 horsepower, and the wilder RPO 579D, which claimed 290-horsepower output. Curiously, Chevrolet charged the same price, $484.20, for each version, but not surprisingly, the higher performance version sold five times as many as the lesser model.

and fiscal excesses, but Mitchell had allies, powerful division executives with "gasoline in their veins." Men like Ed Cole understood that styling sold cars for GM.

Mitchell didn't care for the word "styling." He likened it to being fashionable, where something was "in" one day and "out" the next. He knew that good design lasted forever. Soon after his promotion, Mitchell changed the department's name from styling to design.

Mitchell adopted Earl's technique of giving designers little direction with their assignments. Mitchell's temper also rivaled Earl's, but he added a kind of volatile fickleness.

He routinely flipped design concepts 180 degrees from one encounter to the next. For the 1959 Corvette, Mitchell removed some of the design excesses that had marked Harley Earl's final years at GM. He took off the 1958 chrome trim strips along the trunk lid and rows of washboard-like simulated louvers on the engine hood from that model.

Chevrolet engineering carried over its 290-horsepower V-8 engine and sophisticated four-speed transmission. While the heater was still optional, extra-cost handling packages offered stiffer springs and heavily finned brake drums with roadworthy metallic brake linings. The base price was set at $3,875, but ordering a cruise-ready Corvette with a 245-horsepower 283, Powerglide transmission, power top, radio, heater, sunshades, and other minor options would set you back $5,031—about the same as four years of college tuition. Production for 1957 had nearly doubled that of 1956, and it increased to 9,168 for 1958 and 9,670 for 1959.

"Be Brave"

In 1956, GM hired a young designer, Peter Brock, out of the Los Angeles Art Center College. After his first few assignments, Brock was transferred to work with senior stylist Bob Veryzer in Bob McLean's advanced design research studio, joining designer Chuck Pohlmann, studio engineer Byron Voight, and chief modeler John Bird. Mitchell had gone to the auto show in Turin, Italy, and returned to Detroit excited by several coupes he'd seen there. He announced that he wanted to do a new Corvette for a 1960 production model. He described what he wanted and created a contest within the studios to see whose design came closest. Veryzer established his own theme in a two-word sign he posted in the studio: "Be Brave." Brock was daring, and Mitchell selected his concept for a car known internally as XP-84, the Q-car, to use Chevrolet's new sedan independent rear suspension and other innovations.

"I'd designed the car in coupe form, according to Mitchell's direction," Brock said. "At that point Mitchell said, 'I think we also want to do a roadster.'" Young designers Pohlmann and Brock became friends because they shared similar design philosophies. Pohlmann did a roadster version while Brock continued with details on his coupe. "The two cars were nearly identical," Brock recalled, "except for the crisp horizontal line that formed the car's distinctive shape. Chuck's version, directed by Mitchell, fell away to the back. Mine forced a slight kick-up at the rear."

John Bird created full-sized models of Brock's coupe and Pohlmann's roadster variation. They set the two alongside each other, and Mitchell, Brock, Pohlmann, McLean, and Veryzer compared details. Mitchell decided they would build only the roadster prototype because it would be easier and cheaper to do. "So they took the full-sized clay model roadster," Brock said, "and moved it out of the studio, so it wouldn't be discovered. We referred to it as the XP-96, but that car eventually became the Sting Ray race car, which was built in secret."

Pohlmann finished the production roadster along with Larry Shinoda, a senior designer brought over to Studio X by Bill Mitchell. Shinoda was already an industry veteran when he came to GM in September 1956, having worked at Ford and Packard; he also designed a race car that won the Indy 500. Shinoda did most of the form detailing on the new Corvette, such as the twin windscreens, hood louvers, and side vents. The original lines remained Brock's contribution to the design.

Engineer Byron Voight and modeler John Bird built the Brock/Pohlmann/Shinoda XP-84 coupe on the same 94.5-inch wheelbase that Bob Cumberford and Tony Lapine had developed for the proposed 1958 replacement. This new car used the Q-project transaxle to provide more cockpit room without a large transmission sitting between the driver and passenger. It adopted the same advanced frame and also the independent rear suspension that Cumberford and Lapine had devised.

Peter Brock originally designed the XP-84 coupe with a large single piece of glass for the rear window. The split window went in later. Mitchell imposed the hard line down the roof dividing the rear window because he admired the Bugatti-type 57SC Atlantique. He wanted the elegant French car's flavor on the Sting Ray.

Arkus-Duntov promoted aluminum for engine components such as cylinder heads and also for entire blocks, manifolds, and transmission and differential cases. Aluminum would reduce weight, thereby improving handling and fuel economy of the entire Chevrolet line. Using aluminum, a Duntov Corvette would weigh less than 2,500 pounds. Though he advocated aluminum for engine and drive-train components, Arkus-Duntov pushed Chevrolet to build the Corvette's body out of steel. Chevrolet stuck with plastic for several reasons. Stamping dies for steel cost much more, and retaining contact with plastic companies ensured the earliest possibility of working with new composites.

In December 1957, the Engineering Policy Group saw the Q-Corvette. Under Mitchell's watchful eye, Shinoda added working hatches, and he relocated fuel caps to the left rear fender. Mitchell wanted the front fender scoops reversed, placing them at the rear of the doors. In this location, these blew air primarily onto the rear tires. Mitchell felt this accentuated the "Coke-bottle" taper he wanted for the car. Shinoda followed directions and finished a coupe and convertible, ready for presentation at the board of directors' show that would codify or doom production plans.

> ## In 1960 Chevrolet produced 10,261 Corvettes, cracking the break-even point for the first time in its eight-year life. After Ford enlarged its Thunderbird to seat four, Ed Cole hoped the Corvette would absorb the two-seater enthusiasts who felt betrayed. Alas, there were very few.

Opposite: *Legendary car builder/racer Briggs Cunningham entered three 1960 hardtops in the 24 Hours of Le Mans, specially prepared by Alfred Momo in New York (and with great assistance from Chevrolet's Frank Burrell and Zora Arkus-Duntov). A sister car to this reached 151 miles per hour on the four-mile long Mulsanne straight, while this car finished 8th overall, 1st in its production class. This is the car in which racer John Fitch, who had headed the successful 1956 and 1957 Sebring efforts for Chevrolet, and co-driver Bob Grossman spent 24 hours. Production class rules required both seats and the carpet as well as the roll-bar and hardtop roof in place. Fighting off an overheating engine, they pitted according to the rules, but at each stop they packed the engine compartment with ice. The car was being prepared for numerous vintage races and Corvette 50-year celebrations.*

Around this time, GM underwent a critical personnel change. Company chairman Harlow Curtice retired in 1958. His replacement was Frederic Donner. To Donner, stockbrokers were even more important to GM than shareholders. While Curtice believed that interesting automobiles with a pleasing appearance helped sell cars, Donner believed that reducing costs by curbing the huge expenditures of design and engineering would increase dividends. Profits—not Earl's chrome or Arkus-Duntov's independent rear suspensions—made GM attractive to Wall Street. Experiments like the Sting Ray were frivolous and expensive.

Ed Cole carried over the existing body from the 1958–59 model years for 1960. Chassis engineers tamed the handling by deleting the optional heavy-duty springs while increasing the diameter of the front anti-sway bar and adding a rear one. The $336.60 RPO 687 was really a "PRO" (production racing option). It quickened the steering and fitted sintered-metallic brake linings inside new brake drums cast with large cooling fins. Base price of the car was $3,872. The top engine option was the 1958–59 290-horsepower 283 V-8 with the Duntov cam, solid valve lifters, 11.0:1 compression ratio, and fuel injection.

A Personal Race Car for Bill

Bill Mitchell was a racing enthusiast, although he never competed himself. Mitchell urged along the completion of Jerry Earl's SR-2 in 1956, and later he acquired, for $1, the

1957 SS mule chassis on which Arkus-Duntov had done his brake development work for Sebring. The AMA racing ban covered corporate involvement, but Mitchell saw no problem in being a private race-car owner. He asked designers Larry Shinoda and Ed Wayne to convert the hidden Q-Corvette XP-96 roadster theme into his own personal race car.

Mitchell and Shinoda ran it with a modified 283, similar to the 1957 SS engine, developing 280 horsepower. The first body was 1/8-inch thick fiberglass, nearly production heft, reinforced with aluminum. Dick Thompson premiered the bright red racer at Marlboro Raceway in Maryland in mid-April 1959. Despite a repeat of Sebring's 1957 race with unreliable brakes, too much unrestrained power, and no limited-slip differential, Thompson still managed to finish fourth in the first appearance.

Peter Brock recalled that the car was terrible aerodynamically. "When Thompson first drove the car, the front wheels came off the ground at 140 miles per hour. The lift on the hood was like an airplane wing."

Mitchell's team manager was Dean Bedford, a GM engineer who also supervised the development of the road car. He partially solved the front-lift problem by shimming up the rear springs, creating a nose-down "hot rod rake." This eliminated some, but not all, of the problem. Then the thick body panels cracked from stress. Bedford formed a new nose and tail section of three-layer fiberglass silk reinforced with balsa wood. These thinner panels gave the nose and tail such flexibility that it deformed but popped back when hit. Thompson said they literally waved at high speed; however, it saved 75 pounds compared to the original body. Throughout the season, one problem after another vexed Mitchell, Bedford, sometimes-mechanic Shinoda, and driver Thompson.

During the 1960 season, the car reappeared in silver, with a simpler braking system and a paper-thin fiberglass skin that pulled body weight down to 2,000 pounds. With so many other problems to control, Mitchell, Bedford, and Thompson agreed to a modest 280 horsepower at the flywheel for reliability. With a 3.70:1 rear

Opposite: *Indianapolis Chevrolet dealer Bud Gates had ordered the car with all the racing options, but only when reading the 1961 Sebring 12-hour race rules did he discover that the car needed a hardtop. At the last minute he sent a mechanic out into the new car lot at night to "borrow one". The mechanic took the first one he found, red. Gates and co-driver Harry Heuer ran a sensible race, driving conservatively to a 22nd overall finish, good enough for 2nd in class. After the race, Bud drove the car back home to Indiana, selling it on his high-performance used-car lot 18 months later.*

end, Thompson could see 155 miles per hour on tracks like Bridgehampton and Meadowdale. Thompson put it to good use, thrilling spectators and chasing—but rarely beating—Augie Pabst in his Chevrolet-engined Scarab. Still, long before the last race of the season, Thompson won the C-modified class championship with his consistent, careful driving.

Private racers campaigned Corvettes around the country in 1961, competing rather successfully with a five-car Sebring effort. Delmo Johnson, a Chevy dealer from Dallas, entered three of these, and the other two came from Don Yenko in Cannonsburg, Pennsylvania. At the end of the 12-hour event, Johnson and co-driver Dave Morgan finished 11th overall, the best finish to date for a stock model.

Mitchell retired the car after the 1960 season. It had cost him a fortune, yet it established itself as the racing Corvette. He returned it to design for a complete renovation, where it got new paint and, finally, a Corvette badge.

Previous pages and above: Zora Arkus-Duntov named it the Chevrolet Experimental Racing Vehicle. Despite GM chairman Harlow Curtice's support of the 1957 Automobile Manufacturers Association ban on racing, Arkus-Duntov and his colleagues built it to meet the specifications for the 1960 Indianapolis 500.

It went on the GM show tour, exhibited first at the Chicago automobile show in mid-February 1961. After a year on display platforms, Mitchell took it back to use as his fair-weather commuter car, eventually installing Dunlop disk brakes and a 427-ci engine.

The Sting Ray

As 1960 turned to 1961, Harry Barr's engineers were at work on an enlarged 283 engine, and externally the Corvette changed enough for customers to part with their hard-earned cash for the new model.

"Gene, go down to the basement, you're going to be working with one of the guys on the sports car." That was Gene Garfinkle's introduction to what would become the Sting Ray production design project. He was working in the Buick production studio when one of Mitchell's people came in and sent him to the Corvette.

Garfinkle and Ed Wayne did all the drawings, using Chuck Pohlmann's Sting Ray roadster as a reference. The coupe had its split rear window, modeled on the Bugatti that Mitchell loved. The Sting Ray racing car was brought in to the studio, with the original drawings up on the wall. Garfinkle recalled that Mitchell was in there three or four times a day.

Mitchell continued Harley Earl's practice of producing show cars and design study vehicles to introduce the public to ideas that he and his design staff were considering for future production. While his Sting Ray raced, Mitchell prepared the XP-700, a road-going showpiece, built in 1958. He had taken Cumberford's ideas such as the extended nose and grille from Jerry Earl's SR-2 and pushed them further. The rear end hinted strongly at shapes for the 1961 production car. Its removable hardtop was a transparent plastic bubble, parted in the middle by

a metal strip with air vents down the back and a rearview mirror perched outside on top. When the 1961 car reached dealers, enthusiasts saw a front end only slightly changed from the 1960 car, but the rear end was a successful transfer from Mitchell's XP-700—the next hint of what would be the Corvette in 1963.

Mechanical changes were subtle. Engineering replaced the heavy copper-core radiators with aluminum versions that were half the weight yet provided 10 percent greater capacity, improving weight balance and cooling. Two-thirds of the 1961 buyers ordered the close-ratio four-speed transmission, and about one-fifth still wanted the three-speed manual; the remaining buyers chose the two-speed Powerglide automatic.

In all, Chevrolet produced 10,939 of the 1961 models. The top performance engine was now the 315-horsepower 283-ci V-8 with Rochester fuel injection. Base price was $3,934, and more than half the buyers ordered the optional removable hardtop for an additional $236.75.

Corvette mechanicals had evolved to the point in 1961 where the performance was reliable, its racing pedigree was established, and the car had earned respect. It had reached the stage in its life where outsiders wondered if a Corvette by any other name might smell so sweet, work so well, look so good, or race so successfully.

Chevrolet management changed at the top again in 1961. Semon E. "Bunkie" Knudsen was promoted from the Pontiac division to head GM's biggest seller. Bunkie liked racing, and he understood what the AMA liked to deny: "speed" promoted sales. He ushered out a great amount of parts, support, advice, and money through a back door at Pontiac and into the hands of stock car and drag racers. Knudsen's actions and Pontiac's successes led Ford to publicly repudiate the AMA ban in 1962.

Fort Worth, Texas, entrepreneur Gary B. Laughlin drilled oil, processed petroleum, and owned Chevy dealerships. For pleasure, he raced a Ferrari 750 Monza in SCCA

events, where he met and formed an idea with two other Texan racing buddies, Carroll Shelby and Jim Hall. Hall and Shelby wanted a true GT-version of the Corvette, lighter and possibly lovelier. Laughlin, tired of his huge Ferrari repair bills, offered to finance the project, and Shelby offered to engineer it. Together they'd race them. They hoped to make enough cars to qualify for SCCA's B-production class and planned to sell some to their competitors. Memos flew early in 1959 from Fort Worth to Warren, to Modena, Italy. Sergio Scaglietti, car-body fabricator for Enzo Ferrari, agreed to revise an existing fastback aluminum coupe to fit the Corvette chassis for Laughlin. Three 1959 mechanically complete, bare chassis arrived at Scaglietti.

Laughlin's oil operations took him to Europe regularly, and he always visited Modena. The car got closer to what he wanted. With a Spartan interior, the new aluminum coupes weighed 400 pounds less than the fiberglass production cars.

They completed their first one, painted silver, in early 1961, on a chassis with a 1960 engine, the 290-horsepower 283-ci V-8 with Rochester fuel injection, close-ratio four-speed transmission, and Positraction. Scaglietti refitted the Corvette teeth into the front air intake. His sparse interior contained two thin competition seats facing a crackle-finish instrument panel.

The second prototype was done more luxuriously with an automatic transmission. It was intended for Hall, who was experimenting with racing automatic transmissions. It and the third car, another four-speed transmission version, bore Corvette crossed flags on the nose and egg-crate grilles.

While Laughlin worked with Scaglietti, Wisconsin industrial designer Gordon Kelly began a redesign project with Carrozzeria Vignale on his 1960 Corvette. He produced a 1/8th-scale clay model of a Corvette body and showed it to Bill Mitchell. Mitchell offered Gordon a car if he'd find a builder who would display it at the Paris Auto Show in October 1961. Vignale agreed. Kelly's lines, stubbier but more aggressive than Scaglietti's coupes, were

Previous pages and above: *Chevrolet division manager Ed Cole and Zora Arkus-Duntov both had good experiences testing prototype Corvettes at Pike's Peak, and their goal for the CERV was similar. In early days it was even called "the Hillclimber." Its seat back is very vertical to give the driver excellent visibility, unlike more reclining Grand Prix and Indy car seating positions meant to keep drivers out of the wind.*

striking behind an oversized oval egg-crate grille. The Kelly/Vignale-bodied car appeared in auto shows for a year before Kelly finally got to drive the car and test its fuel-injected 283, the RPO 687 brakes and suspension option, four-speed transmission, and Positraction differential.

The 1962 Corvette introduced another legendary power plant. Harry Barr's engineers started with the 283-ci V-8 and increased the displacement to 327 cubic inches. The base engine produced 250 horsepower, while the solid lifter, Duntov-cam, fuel-injected engine developed 360 horsepower. The most powerful optional engine still cost $484.20, the same price since 1958. A car ready for racing ran $5,243, while a civilized cruiser with every comfort option sold for $5,014 in 1962.

A New Challenge

Corvette designers and engineers tackled the few lingering criticisms, improving the perceptions that sports-car enthusiasts held about Corvettes. Yet Chevrolet's only remaining competitor—Jaguar—did not rest either. The English firm accepted that the V-8 was necessary for most American buyers, but a dual-overhead camshaft on top of a proven inline six-cylinder engine would turn heads on their side of the Atlantic Ocean. Packaging it in a stunning body form would help even more.

Jaguar introduced its new 1962 XK-E in the spring of 1961 at the New York Auto Show, 18 months before GM could show the new Sting Ray. Jaguar's slender coupe and roadster presented a new challenge to Corvette. As Briggs Cunningham had predicted, the U.S. had become the world's largest market for sports cars. Jaguar sold most of its cars on this side of the pond. The new body on its new chassis, with independent rear suspension and four-wheel disc brakes, would sell for $4,915.

For the GM brass, engineers, and designers, the Jaguar XK-E meant a little more running in place, hurrying to get the last of the work perfect before everybody in the world could see what they'd been working on for the last seven years.

THE CORVETTE: WORLD-CLASS SPORTS CAR

CHAPTER FIVE

chapter five

THE CORVETTE: WORLD CLASS SPORTS CAR 1963–1967

The 1963 Sting Ray etched Bill Mitchell's influence and power into GM's corporate granite. Peter Brock's coupe, finished by Mitchell's lieutenant, Larry Shinoda, paid homage to the classic "boat-tail" roadsters from the 1930s. By now, Mitchell's power nearly rivaled that of Harley Earl. When Zora Arkus-Duntov complained that the center spine in the window hindered rearward vision, Mitchell retorted, "If you take that off, you might as well forget the whole thing." Corvette was making money, and because Earl's department had created it, the car belonged to design, not to engineering. Mitchell had the highest authority, and he made it clear that engineering's input was accepted when it did not interfere.

Engineering made the new car as impressive mechanically as it was visually. The car benefited from the Q-Corvette project, from Mitchell's Sting Ray race car, and from Zora's pet project, the CERV I (Chevrolet Engineering Research Vehicle).

Previous Pages and Opposite: *Bill Mitchell enjoyed teasing the public as much as Harley Earl did, and this New York and Chicago auto show model continued the tradition. While it was basically a 1963 Sting Ray convertible, it picked the exterior exhaust headers and side pipes from the 1961 SP-755 Shark show car.*

Chevrolet produced 199 Z06 models, yet careful study of Mike Antonick's Corvette Black Book *suggests that fewer than this number were inteded to race. Chevrolet delivered only 124 cars without radios and just 63 with the 36-gallon fuel tank. Admittedly,only those planning outings at Sebring and Daytona benefited from the big tanks; for shorter club races the extra capacity would be wasted.*

They settled on a 98-inch wheelbase for the production Sting Ray, internally known as the XP-720. This was shorter than the previous car's XK-120 dimension of 102 inches, thus improving maneuverability and handling. Using a new ladder-type frame with five cross-members to replace the original car's X-frame, engineers dropped the center of gravity nearly 2.3 inches because the new frame now let them place passengers inside the frame rails rather than on top of them.

Engineering had a limited budget, and Arkus-Duntov wanted to use the new rear axle with fully independent rear suspension (IRS). They could devise one from the Q-sedans and Q-Corvette prototype. Engineering had done the development work years before and wrote off the costs against other budgets, but GM chairman Frederic Donner killed the production passenger car, so there was no big project to pay for it. Whenever Arkus-Duntov stated his need for an IRS, the newly important bean counters challenged him on its cost. Arkus-Duntov already knew the car business was a numbers game. He prevailed by telling the bean counters that the new Corvette with IRS would sell 30,000 units, even though most drivers would never recognize the difference.

The system devised by Arkus-Duntov and his engineering staff also adopted technology from the CERV I. It incorporated twin half shafts that emerged from a frame-mounted differential, connected (and suspended) by a transversely mounted nine-leaf spring bolted to the back of the differential housing. A transverse spring hadn't been used on any U.S. automobile since the front suspension on the 1937 Cord. Arkus-Duntov's system used the drive shafts as part of the suspension system, and it weighed much less than the 1962 solid tube rear axle.

Engineering carried over the front suspension with subtle changes, using mostly passenger car production

Above and opposite: *By the time Gulf Oil's Grady Davis picked up his Z06 to campaign at Sebring and Daytona, Zora Arkus-Duntov had already begun working on Sting Ray prototype racers called Grand Sports. As a result, Grand Sport bits and pieces such as larger rear brakes, air cooling ducts, and front hood wind deflectors were available to Z06 competitors.*

parts that had appeared in new configurations on the CERV I. A faster steering ratio was used to improve road feel, steering response, and ride comfort. The Sting Ray also introduced power steering, available on all but the two most powerful engine options.

The development dollars were nearly gone, so engineering carried over the 11-inch-diameter cast-iron drum brakes all around. Buyers could order optional sintered-metallic linings and finned aluminum brake drums that

provided greater fade resistance and better cooling. Power-assisted brakes were also an option.

Once all the new technology was gathered together, engineering built development mules. Arkus-Duntov and his associates used these for daily transport, living with their work and making constant adjustments. Concurrently, Bill Mitchell devised another show car that he could drive.

Mitchell again called on Larry Shinoda, who had done all the production drawings for the Sting Ray and knew its lines better than anyone. Mitchell gave him a new project number, XP-755, and described a design theme that had come to him while fishing in the Caribbean. His first Corvette was the Sting Ray and his new car would be the Shark with a paint scheme to match. Shinoda adopted the strongest features of Mitchell's Sting Ray racer and of the upcoming production car, exaggerating some of them. He included the double-bubble glass top from Mitchell's first show car, the XP-700.

Leonard McLay had kept Harley Earl's supercharged Buick LeSabre running. Over time he tamed a great number of temperamental engines. He and his crew supercharged a 327 for Mitchell's new car. Over its 10-year life, the Shark's engine compartment "tested" power-steering pumps, power-brake boosters, and a 427-ci displacement Mark IV engine. Mitchell first showed it at the New York Auto Show in April 1962.

A Sports Car With Luggage Room

Designers created a new instrument panel and gauge cluster that gave the tachometer and speedometer equal importance, and the steering column offered 3 inches of length adjustment. Designers and engineers created a large luggage storage area behind the seats in the coupe that was only accessible from the inside. It was the Sting Ray body that seized viewers' attention.

The GM board approved the full-size clay coupe body in April 1960 and the interior in November. Mitchell reluctantly created a convertible in the fall after being told to do so. Once the board committed to building the new car in fiberglass, engineering and design collaborated to make the new body stronger, tighter, and quieter. A rotating housing was developed to overcome the wind resistance that quad headlights generated. The wrap-over,

This page and following pages: *Front and rear differentials ran at slightly different final drive ratios to ensure proper power delivery. Under hard acceleration, the less heavily weighted front tires spun faster than the rears. The multi-disc clutch and automatic transmissions later proved indomitable when Texan Jim Hall adapted them to his sports racing Chaparrals. His earliest racers even resembled the CERV II.*

No matter how many years it has been since its introduction, the Sting Ray coupe's boat-tail body still strikes automobile-design enthusiasts as a thing of beauty.

limousine-style doors launched a new design trend and greatly improved entry and exit. Shinoda drew in working vents on the hood and behind the doors, but with design and development funds depleted, there was nothing left to make the air-ventilation plumbing work.

Zora Arkus-Duntov cautiously commented that private customers would race Corvettes whether GM approved or not. As plans advanced for Sting Ray production, he continued to suggest it was in Chevrolet's best interest to carry on parts development to benefit racers. His hunch was correct, especially when Ford's Total Performance Program in 1962 effectively returned them to racing. Arkus-Duntov made sure Corvette racers were ready.

Zora Arkus-Duntov and his cohorts created RPO Z06. This Special Performance Equipment package included heavy-duty vacuum-boosted brakes, a larger diameter front anti-sway bar, larger shocks, and much stiffer springs. Initially, the package fit a 36.5-gallon gas tank instead of the new 20-gallon container. It also included the 360-horsepower 327 engine, M-21 close-ratio four-speed transmission, Positraction, and cast-aluminum

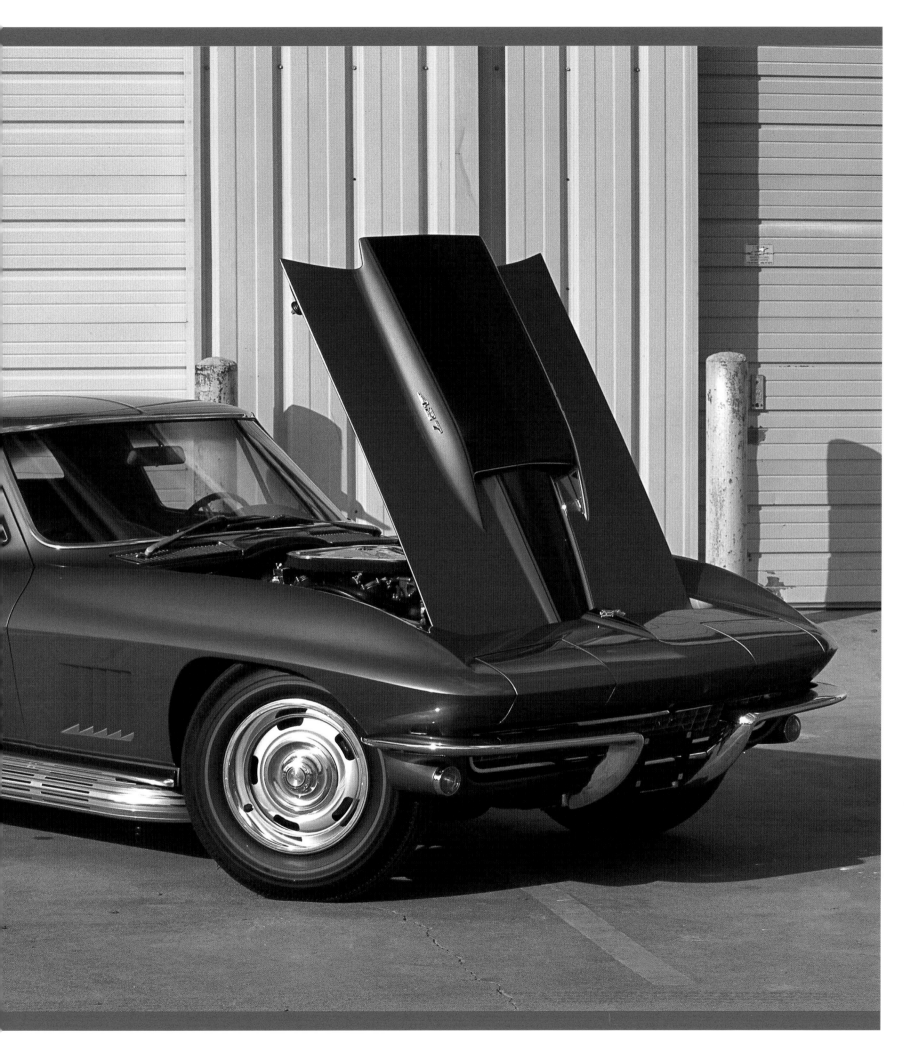

While badges and louvers either disappeared or became totally functional, one new design flourish appeared. Chevrolet's 427-ci big-block engines now fit under a non-functional scoop set off with contrasting color paint.

knock-off wheels. The Z06 package cost buyers an extra $1,818.45 over the base coupe price of $4,257. Initially, buyers could order the package only for coupes, since the oversize tank wouldn't fit the convertible. It was a pricey race-ready package. Deleting the heater and defroster saved $100, but the total tipped in at $5,975.45. Later in the model year, problems were discovered with air leaking

through the porous aluminum castings. The knock-off wheels and the extra-large gas tank were deleted from the package, although the tank was available on any coupe separately. The price was lowered to $1,293.95 for the package, and it was available for the convertible as well. Chevrolet produced 199 Z06s.

Production began just as Bill Mitchell introduced his Shark in New York. Crews working inside the plant but outside the regular production line manufactured about 25 pilot 1963 models by late June and quickly parceled them out to enthusiast magazines so they could publish their stories at the same time dealers unveiled the new

car. "The 1963 Corvette," *Road & Track* publisher John Bond wrote, "has come a long way in 10 years—from a stylist's plaything to a full-blown, out-and-out dual-purpose sports car." In general, the automotive press loved the new Corvette.

Chevrolet announced double shifts at the St. Louis plant late in the fall. The production goal for the 1963 model was 16,000 units. When the counting was done, they had sold 10,594 coupes and 10,919 convertibles, a total of 21,513 cars. Not quite the 30,000 Arkus-Duntov had predicted, but the sales figures far exceeded Chevrolet's own estimations, and it beat 1962 sales by nearly 50 percent.

The Muscle Car Wars

The Corvette's split rear window was dropped for 1964, as were the nonfunctional hood grilles. Engines got stronger with the addition of Holley 4150 carburetors, and peak power of the solid-lifter engine rose from 340 to 365 horsepower. Engineering provided a new intake manifold for the fuel-injected version, increasing output to 375 horsepower.

Another group within General Motors, hungry for Corvette's performance image, started looking in a new direction. Pontiac launched the Tempest Le Mans and

It could be promoted as a weight-saving improvement. The RPO L89 aluminum cylinder heads fitted onto the L71 427 cast-iron block, cutting 75 pounds off the front end, taking engine weight down to within 40 pounds of a fully equipped 327. A Car and Driver road test saw 13.6-second quarter-mile times, at 105 miles per hour. The lighter weight improved handling as well.

Corvette Wins

In racing, Arkus-Duntov's Z06 coupes proved formidable in their first outing, at the Los Angeles Times Three-Hour Invitational Race at Riverside, California, in October 1962. Bob Bondurant, Dave MacDonald, and Jerry Grant drove the three cars out from the St. Louis factory to break them in, and a fourth was trucked out. From the start, the event quickly became a contest between MacDonald in his Z06 and one of Carroll Shelby's new cars. After Chevrolet declined to sell him cars without bodies, Shelby took his idea to Ford. Upon hearing Chevrolet's reaction, Ford gave Shelby all the engines and help he needed. Shelby stuffed Ford V-8s into the English AC Ace and renamed the car the Cobra. Bill Krause raced the Cobra hard. Both MacDonald's Z06 and Krause's Cobra broke after the first hour, and two more Corvettes retired by the end of the second. The fourth Corvette, entered by Mickey Thompson and driven by Doug Hooper, won the race.

Shelby's Cobra won the A-production championship by June, but Arkus-Duntov remained philosophical. Though disappointed, he knew that under current GM management the Cobra was insignificant. Donner cared about the pocketbooks of thousands of customers who never raced cars.

GTO options in 1963 and 1964. These were compact cars stuffed with 389-ci "tri-power" engines fueled by three two-barrel carburetors. The small cars were cheap to build and therefore inexpensive to purchase. They cost thousands less than a fully optioned Corvette, yet they went just as fast at the stoplight-to-stoplight drag races that took place every Saturday night on any main street. These big engines began pulling the Corvette away from Arkus-Duntov's goals for the car. Yet Chevrolet's general manager, Bunkie Knudsen, fresh from Pontiac himself, felt the Corvette could not be left out of this new definition of sporting cars. Big engines were inevitable.

Total Corvette production in 1964 reached another record, 22,229 cars, including 8,304 coupes and 13,925 convertibles. Chevrolet held the 1963 prices, keeping the coupe at $4,252 and the convertible at $4,037. The 1964 racers' package, now assembled from a variety of RPOs rather that a single one, set the buyer back a total of $6,526.40, a price that included the 375-horsepower "fuelie." By comparison, a 389-ci dual-quad, fully performance-optioned Pontiac GTO coupe cost less than $3,800.

Design did more with erasers than pencils for 1965, eliminating hood and roof vents while opening the former "speedlines" behind the front tires to make real working vents. It was a mid-1965 engine introduction that put the Corvette back on track against the competition.

When Jim Premo succeeded Harry Barr as Chevrolet's chief engineer, he found vigorous supporters in Bunkie Knudsen and Zora Arkus-Duntov. Everyone knew Corvettes would get the larger engines being pursued by Pontiac and others. Arkus-Duntov's high-performance engine group had been working on its own solution to that inevitability.

A board policy limited intermediate-size cars—Chevrolet's Chevelle, Pontiac's Tempest, and the like—to engine displacements below 400 cubic inches. With that in mind, the engine developers produced the Mark IV big-block motor with a 396-ci displacement.

Released in mid-1965, this powerhouse engine was dubbed the L78, with 425 horsepower on tap. The rating was conservative, as a number of enthusiasts discovered when they had their engines blueprinted. Available as an option for only $292.70, some 2,157 Corvette buyers exercised the option. The price included a visual cue: a new hood that swelled in the center in a "power bulge" to

Charlie Snyder from Astoria, New York, ordered an L71-equipped convertible with the hardtop to run in AHRA local and regional races. Snyder took the car directly to Motion Performance after picking it up from Baldwin

Chevrolet in February 1967. Very quickly Charlie began winning races, and he made a name for himself and the car, routinely running 11.5 seconds at 124 miles per hour.

An incoming mortar round killed 19-year-old Charlie within a month of his arriving in Vietnam. His mother and sister put the car in a garage until a year later when Motion Performance owner Joel Rosen and Baldwin parts manager John Mahler asked if they could continue to race the car in Charlie's name.

accommodate the engine's bulk. Option N14 was even more visible. This $134.50 package put exhaust pipes along the side of the car, as seen on countless Bill Mitchell show cars. Only 759 buyers had the nerve to announce so clearly to local police what they intended.

The muscle power wars turned serious in 1966. By the end of 1965, Chevrolet division had a new chief executive,

Elliott M. "Pete" Estes, replacing Knudsen. While with the Pontiac division, Estes and collaborator John DeLorean had intensified, if not invented, the muscle car.

Engineering stretched the Mark IV closer to its full potential by increasing bore to 4.25 inches, raising displacement to 427 ci. It was offered in two versions. The first was the L36, with a single four-barrel carburetor and hydraulic lifters to achieve 390-horsepower output. The higher-output L72 with mechanical lifters was quoted at 425 horsepower, an extremely conservative rating. The engine transformed the Corvette. Runs from 0 to 60 miles per hour took a scant 4.8 seconds, and the car hit 100

More Stopping Power

Years of battling over costs and arguing about their benefits finally paid off in 1965 when engineering was able to provide four-wheel disc brakes on the Corvette at no extra cost. Chevrolet engineering insisted that brake performance had to be measurably better than its drums, particularly by providing superior "braking feel." Chevrolet engineers worked with Delco-Moraine to devise a new approach. In their system, pads barely touched the disc at all times. This provided instant pedal response and alleviated an early problem: when the rotors got wet, they were less effective than drums. Designing the caliper so the pads floated against the rotor swept it clean of moisture and road grit. Similar to what it did with the Z06 package in 1963, engineering fit the dual master cylinder as standard equipment on all disc-brake-equipped cars.

miles per hour only 11.2 seconds after leaving the line. The changes were not lost on the performance-conscious public. Corvette had another banner sales year in 1966, with 9,958 coupes and 17,762 convertibles sold.

The 1967 model turned out to be the best Sting Ray yet. Delays in production engineering once again held up a replacement, so mild design updates would have to do. Under the hood, however, the changes were far more substantial. New code numbers entered Corvette order books: L71, the 427-ci V-8 with a trio of progressively linked two-barrel carburetors that produced 435 horsepower. Some 3,754 buyers paid $437.10 to follow this route. Savvy buyers got an option on the optional engine by checking L89, which fitted aluminum cylinder heads on the L71; only 16 of these were delivered, at an additional $368.65 over the engine cost.

One new engine code became legendary: L88, a 427-ci engine with 12.5:1 compression. Chevrolet engineering knew what it had. Hoping to prevent people from buying something far beyond their abilities, the company dis-

couraged unknowing buyers by quoting 430 horsepower, five less than the lesser L-71, yet doubling its price to $947.90. Topped by a single Holley carburetor sucking 850 cubic feet of air per minute and demanding a diet of 103-octane fuel, the true output of this engine was closer to 560 horsepower. Buyers could only get the car with transistorized ignition, Positraction, F41 suspension, and J50 power brakes. Ordering the engine automatically deleted the heater and radio, "to cut down on weight and discourage the car's use on the street," according to a release at introduction. Only 20 individuals paid for this option, many of them seeing it for what it was: a flat-out racing engine with a regular production option code.

The first of the engines appeared in late 1966, slipping out the back door to select competitors. Chevrolet's director of promotions, Vince Piggins, was more accurately the division's director of racing. To help performance customers, he created an ordering system, the Central Office Purchase Order (COPO), to take advantage of what he knew Arkus-Duntov and others were doing in the back rooms.

By June, Piggins had commandeered a 1967 preproduction car, and he helped California dealer Peyton Cramer obtain the first 1967 L88 coupe to take to Le Mans. Cramer, who owned Dana Chevrolet, knew racing; he had been Carroll Shelby's general manager at Shelby American. Although the L88 weighed 300 pounds more than the closest competitor in the GT class, Dick Guldstrand, Cramer's high-performance manager, and Bob Bondurant, now Dana's regular driver in SCCA and Can-Am entries, clocked it at 171.5 miles per hour on the Mulsanne Straight, 22 miles per hour faster than the nearest GT Ferrari. Sadly, the blistering pace took its toll and the L88 expired after 11 hours, leaving the slower Ferrari to win GT.

Though Chevrolets had raced on NASCAR ovals, road courses, drag strips, and across the salt flats at Bonneville in Utah, by the time the Sting Ray appeared, the division had adopted an unofficial and unspoken snobbery. It held that Corvettes belonged on road courses, while Impalas, Chevelles, or Camaros could drag race or go fender-to-fender around the ovals. Corvettes already had a reputation among drag racers for being expensive to buy and race and fragile to operate because they broke down regularly. Racers such as Bo Laws and Dick Moroso had another view. They said the car " 'hooks' like nobody's business." Despite the car's drawbacks, a few drag racers made their place in history racing Sting Rays.

On Long Island, New York, Baldwin Chevrolet and Joel Rosen's Motion Performance had a working relationship with Vince Piggins, who helped get them parts and engines. Rosen created 427-engined "Stage III" muscle Chevrolets. When he heard from Piggins that the L88 would be available in a box in midsummer 1967, he ordered two through Baldwin's parts manager John Mahler. Rosen and Mahler knew at least one likely customer.

Charlie Snyder was born and raised in nearby Astoria, and the 20-year-old loved racing. In early February 1967, he took delivery of a Marlboro Maroon convertible with the 425-horsepower 427-ci engine. To protect himself from outrageous insurance rates in car theft–prone Queens, he titled the car in his mother's name, Grace Snyder. He drove the car straight to Rosen for tuning and modification.

Over the next several months, "Astoria Chas," as he became known, drove to the track, raced, and won, regularly turning 11.5-second times at 124 miles per hour. He also ran after midnights on the connecting highways in Queens, where crowds lined the roadway three deep to see racing under the street lights. Rosen's increased power and torque eventually twisted the chassis. Snyder ordered a replacement, and the car sat for a month in a service bay at Baldwin. Rosen's two L88s were on the same truckload with Snyder's chassis, and he wasted no time securing one of the two. Baldwin's mechanics gusset-welded the chassis to handle the additional power. Over the next few weeks, Snyder raced regularly and won repeatedly in the car he named "Ko-Motion."

After a spring and summer of hard running, Charlie had to replace the chassis, which had twisted from the torque. Later, his factory original 427-ci 435 horsepower L71 engine expired. Snyder learned through Joel Rosen that L88 engines with aluminum heads would be available in crates. Snyder took one of the first two Rosen got, likely to be the first L88s in private hands.

Snyder was drafted into the army in the winter of 1967. In the spring of 1968, on leave after basic training, he returned to Queens, repainted the graphics on his car, and raced several more times. Then he was sent to Vietnam. One month after arriving, he died of injuries from an exploding mortar round. Back home, his Corvette sat in Grace's garage throughout the 1968 summer season while his family grieved the loss of their only son.

After a year passed, Mahler and Rosen approached Grace Snyder about racing the car again. They said they would cover all its expenses, running it "in memory of Astoria Chas." It had been Charlie's dream to set an AHRA record, and she agreed to let them run the car. Mahler and Rosen prepped the car that winter and resumed racing in the spring of 1969 with Bill Foster, a local pro, behind the wheel. The car made headlines, running 11.04-second elapsed times at 129 miles per hour and winning the A/Corvette World Record in Charlie Snyder's name.

Mahler and Rosen made one final modification to the car. They changed the heads and mounted an 850-cfm Holley carburetor. With this set up, Mahler pulled a 10.74 time at National Speedway in Queens, registering the accomplishment in Charlie's name. The next afternoon, with the time whitewashed in shoe polish on the window and trophies stuffed into the foot wells, Rosen and Mahler trailered the car to the home of Charlie's sister Sharon. They pushed it into her garage and covered it, where it remained for 30 years, one of a handful of Corvette drag-racing legends.

COMPANY RACING CROSSES THE FINISH LINE FOR THE LAST TIME

CHAPTER SIX

chapter six

COMPANY RACING CROSSES THE FINISH LINE FOR THE LAST TIME

1963–1967

Bunkie Knudsen liked seeing his cars in the spotlight. He knew that in October 1962 a Corvette Z06 had beaten Carroll Shelby's new Cobra at Riverside Raceway. Arkus-Duntov's description of Shelby's car made its potential clear to Knudsen. He encouraged Arkus-Duntov to be discrete but to think as ambitiously as Ford and Shelby.

Arkus-Duntov understood that the FIA's recent rule changes, which made Grand Touring cars eligible in the World Championship for auto-makers, was a subtly worded invitation to U.S. manufacturers. He also recognized that entering his mid-engine CERV II four-wheel-drive

Previous Pages: *In early 1965, Notre Dame University engineering student Tony De Lorenzo had volunteered to help classmates find interesting cars for a campus auto show. Tony called his father, who worked at GM at the time, and asked him if there was anything interesting in design or engineering that they could send. Dad visited Arkus-Duntov and Mitchell. The unpainted #002 Grand Sport roadster got a coat of "Mitchell blue" and was sent to the show.*

Opposite: *Chevrolet dealer Dick Doane first raced chassis #003, using a nearly stock 327-ci 360 horsepower cast iron engine. At the Road America 500 in September 1963, Doane blew up the engine after 92 laps. The car returned to Chevrolet to prepare it for Nassau Speed Weeks. For Nassau, the car got a quick fill gas cap and wider fenders to house 11-inch Halibrand wheels and Goodyear tires for John Mecom's racing effort.*

coupe in Le Mans in 1964 was not discrete. He knew what it took to win the French race outright, having won his class there in a Porsche 550 Spyder some years earlier.

Arkus-Duntov considered a "lightweight" 1,800-pound Corvette. He would need 600 horsepower to propel the car with its aerodynamic faults. He and fellow engineer Walt Zetye fabricated an aluminum chassis that saved 94 pounds over steel. Then they transferred the IRS that Zetye devised for the CERV, and which would later appear on the production Sting Ray. They used a Dana-limited slip rear, in an aluminum differential case, to replace the GM Positraction. The body was shortened from 175.3 inches to 172.8 inches and lightened considerably by using paper-thin fiberglass laid over an aluminum substructure. Overall height grew 2 inches but ground clearance dropped from 7.4 inches to 4.3 inches. Because the race car weighed nearly 1,000 pounds less than the production car, Arkus-Duntov decided to try four Girling disc brakes.

FIA racing regulations for 1963 placed no limits on engine displacement, another subtle invitation to the Americans. Engineering's 427 Mark II "mystery motor" could produce the power Arkus-Duntov wanted, but it weighed too much. Boring out an all-aluminum 327-ci block might meet the same ends through different means. A 4-inch stroke and a 4-inch bore gave him a lightweight engine with a displacement of 402 cubic inches. This engine was assembled and tested, then discarded because it was too stressed. A 3.75-inch stroke yielded a less stressful engine displacement of 377 cubic inches. Arkus-Duntov produced three prototype dual-overhead cam versions of this motor that produced 550 horsepower, close enough to his 600 horsepower target to go with it.

Arkus-Duntov took this first car, now known as the Grand Sport (GS), to Sebring in mid-December 1962. Equipped with a race-prepared 327-ci engine, he used it for shakedown runs and tire testing with Firestone and Mickey Thompson. The GS outshined Thompson's purely production-based car, but the Girling brakes proved inadequate. As they replaced the Girling rotors with new ventilated

Throughout the summer of 1963, Arkus-Duntov developed his aluminum-block 377-cubic-inch V-8. He installed these with four 58mm side-draft Weber carburetors into each of Mecom's "private" Grand Sports, #003 (shown here), #004, and #005. (Number 001 and 002 remained with Chevrolet.) The engine developed 485 horsepower at 6,000 rpm, but its tall induction system required a higher hood. Then in March 1965, Arkus-Duntov created a 427 that would literally lift the front tires off the ground in all four gears.

discs, word came down from the corporation. Arkus-Duntov's efforts were too visible behind Donner's back.

Chevrolet had already filed specification papers with the FIA in Paris two weeks before Donner issued an edict halting Arkus-Duntov's program. To qualify for the "Grand Touring" Group III category, the FIA required 100 identical cars constructed by June 1, 1963.

Arkus-Duntov had intended to produce 125 "production" cars for sale to customers to meet the FIA homologation (legalization) requirement. According to the original plan, 1,000 street-legal production cars would follow for public sale later on.

Knudsen, however, had authorized building only 25 cars total, and just 40 of the special 377-ci motors. It was clear now that Donner would never allow manufacture of 25 lightweight Corvettes. In fact, the five prototypes that Arkus-Duntov already had underway were to be "scrapped, sold, or used as testing and evaluation vehicles." Corvettes would not race—at least not corporately. In a heartbeat, the Grand Sport project was done, killed by corporate politics.

Dick Doane, an Illinois car dealer and racer, and Grady Davis, vice president of Gulf Oil and an enthusiastic race driver, were the beneficiaries of Donner's edict. Arkus-Duntov

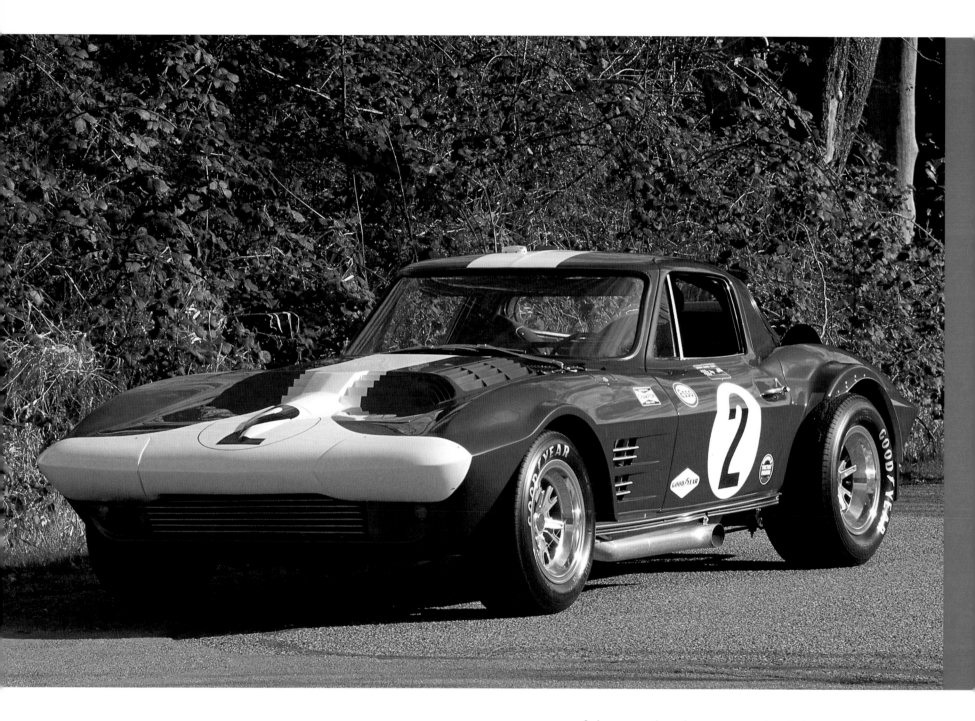

Above and Opposite: *The Z06s raced as production cars, so Arkus-Duntov's idea was to produce Grand Sports that, properly developed, would compete against the world's finest prototypes. Chairman Frederick Donner upheld the 1957 AMA racing ban and cancelled the project just as it became visible.*

sent one of the completed cars to each of them, on loan, with instructions to keep their activities "low key" and not cause Chevrolet any embarrassment. Both cars were white, and Arkus-Duntov equipped them with production stock 360-horsepower 327-ci fuel-injected engines.

Because Arkus-Duntov had built only five, the cars did not qualify for production racing classes, but instead had to go up against modified sports racers like Jim Hall's Chaparrals and Lance Reventlow's Scarabs. This class elevation, however, allowed Doane and Davis to build real racing engines.

Grady Davis put Dr. Dick Thompson in his car. After a shaky start, Thompson and Davis had the car sorted out so well that by early June it consistently finished fifth or better overall. When the SCCA totaled the points, Thompson finished fourth for the year in the C-modified category.

This frustrated Chevrolet engineers and Knudsen, who knew how close they had been with the car. The byword around Chevrolet had been "discrete," but now through Chevrolet's back halls, another word was whispered in a few ears: escalate.

Texas oil heir John Mecom Jr. had begun running a Cooper-engined sports racer, the Xerex Special. He had acquired the car, its builder, Roy Gane, and its driver, Roger Penske, and during the 1963 season he added Augie Pabst and A. J. Foyt to his stable. The team was highly regarded, thoroughly professional, and extremely successful. Because Mecom was a newcomer, he owed allegiance to no one yet, making him the perfect team owner for Chevrolet's whispered plans.

Arkus-Duntov arranged to ship Mecom several engines to install in a variety of sports racers. He called back the

In advance of the December 1963 Nassau Speed Week races, Texas oil heir John Mecom got involved with Chevrolet's racing. Mecom hired drivers Roger Penske, A. J. Foyt, and Augie Pabst. For Chevrolet, this newcomer represented the perfect unrecognized foil to challenge Carroll Shelby's Ford-powered and well-supported Cobras.

Grand Sports he had given to Doane and Davis. He pulled a third car from the garage and set to preparing them for the Nassau Speed Week in December 1963. He had Knudsen's unwritten but enthusiastic blessing.

New body modifications accommodated 11-inch-wide Halibrand wheels, necessary to fit the Mickey Thompson–inspired wide, low-profile Goodyear racing tires. Arkus-Duntov's staff improved ventilation to engine and driver by liberally perforating the car nose, hood, sides, and rear. They dropped in the 377-ci aluminum engines originally developed for the car with their four two-barrel Weber side-draft carburetors. Arkus-Duntov's dynamometers registered 485 horsepower.

Arkus-Duntov had the three Corvettes, chassis 003, 004, and 005, painted blue and shipped to Nassau for arrival on November 30, the day before the first race. Not so coincidentally, several Chevrolet engineers arrived, all vacationing at the same time. Along with the Grand Sports, Mecom sent his three mid-engined Chevrolet-powered sports racers, a Lola GT, a Cooper-Monaco, and a Scarab. Arkus-Duntov felt that if the Corvette Grand Sports did not win, at least a Chevrolet engine was likely to come in first.

The Corvettes won the five-lap qualifying race, but Mecom's Lola took the 99-mile Tourist Trophy on December 1. The Grand Sports' final drives, not broken in before the races, couldn't handle the torque of the 485-horsepower engines or the pounding of the old airport course. Another Chevrolet engineer was suddenly overcome with the need for a Caribbean vacation. He flew down with carefully seasoned rear axles in his baggage.

The second weekend's 112-mile Governors Cup was a better show. A. J. Foyt won in Mecom's Chevy-engined Scarab, and the Grand Sports finished third (Roger Penske), fourth (Augie Pabst), and sixth (Dick Thompson), beating Shelby's best placed Cobra by two spots. The next day's finale, the 252-Mile Nassau Trophy, ended with Dick Thompson in fourth, a Cobra in seventh, and new Mecom-inductee John Cannon in eighth. This longer race, however, pointed out once again the foul aerodynamics of the cars. Air pressure

When GM Chairman Frederick Donner shut down the Grand Sport program, he issued orders to destroy Chevrolet engineering's two remaining cars: #001 and #002. Yet friends of the project hid the cars until 1966 when Roger Penske learned they were available. He bought #001, recommending this car, #002, to his long-time friend George Wintersteen.

built up under the hoods and continually blew the fasteners. Each driver endured several pit stops to cut in new vent holes and apply tape to the panels.

Somehow Nassau escaped Donner's eyes, at least temporarily. The Grand Sport operation returned to Warren for further improvements and modifications before the 1964 season openers at Daytona and Sebring. Engineers fitted a new Rochester fuel-injection system to even out the engine power curve, and they installed a pneumatic-air jacking system to speed pit-stop tire changes. These changes benefited the Mecom team at both venues.

Daytona was a track where maximum speed was beneficial, as it would be at Le Mans and a few other circuits in

the world. A sports-racer body like Mecom's other cars, or like Arkus-Duntov's planned CERV II, would have been ideal—but those would introduce all new development problems. Instead, Arkus-Duntov decided to cut down the brick-like body of the Grand Sport to pick up speed. He removed the roofs from two coupes, chassis 001 and 002, and replaced the tall windshields with low windscreens.

Spies were loose in the back halls at GM, however, and Bunkie Knudsen was called in for a chat with his bosses. A press release announced that Chevrolet was not associated with John Mecom Racing in any way.

Chevrolet quickly sold the three coupes, two to Mecom and one to Jim Hall. Arkus-Duntov had the two

roadsters wrapped under covers and buried in storage. The three coupes began an odyssey of owners, races, and modifications, providing tales that have filled other entire books. The cars campaigned privately, valiantly, and with some success for another three seasons, beating the best that Ford could throw at them.

To Race or Not

Peter Brock moved back to the West Coast in late 1962, joining Shelby's organization. Decades later, he recalled the racing controversy at GM. "The dilemma to race or not split the GM board of directors. In the boardroom the

It was pure and simple, with a 200-miles-per-hour speedometer. The driver's seat adjusted while the passenger's was bolted in place. Because these cars raced in C-Modified class, they never had a chance to prove their potential, always outrun by pure sports racers with similar power but even less weight. Since there were only five Grand Sports, they became instant legends.

battle lines were redrawn: bean counters versus engineers and marketing experts."

Brock observed that neither group seemed capable of convincing the other that they were right. Both sides did agree that Shelby's Cobras were too strong and only a new Chevrolet racer could meet Ford's challenge. It was clear to everyone that any solution would be costly. While they could afford to meet the challenge, the question was whether or not it was worth it.

Donner would not consider risking public embarrassment by circumventing the AMA ban with a racing effort in Europe, as had been suggested by some. He understood that little projects like this kept his engineers excited and loyal, and he would turn a blind eye as long as the activities didn't cast the company in a bad light with the public. Yet the Grand Sports simply could not be. The corporation, he believed, should not spend the money.

In a masterful stroke of public relations, Donner turned a purely economic decision into a safety issue. He was still smarting from the Ralph Nader investigations and congressional subcommittee questions on Corvair safety, during which he had blurted out that GM spent less than one percent of its profits on safety-related research. It was an awful moment. The Grand Sport was the perfect project for him to shut down as a way to improve his reputation. In the newspapers, it would read as purity of motive: Donner was upholding the AMA speed and racing ban even if no one else did. In the eyes of the wary public, he had begun to redeem himself and GM. In the eyes of Wall Street stockbrokers, always far more important to Donner, he had exercised fiscal responsibility.

GOODBYE MIDYEARS, HELLO SHARKS

CHAPTER SEVEN

chapter seven

GOODBYE MIDYEARS, HELLO SHARKS

1968–1982

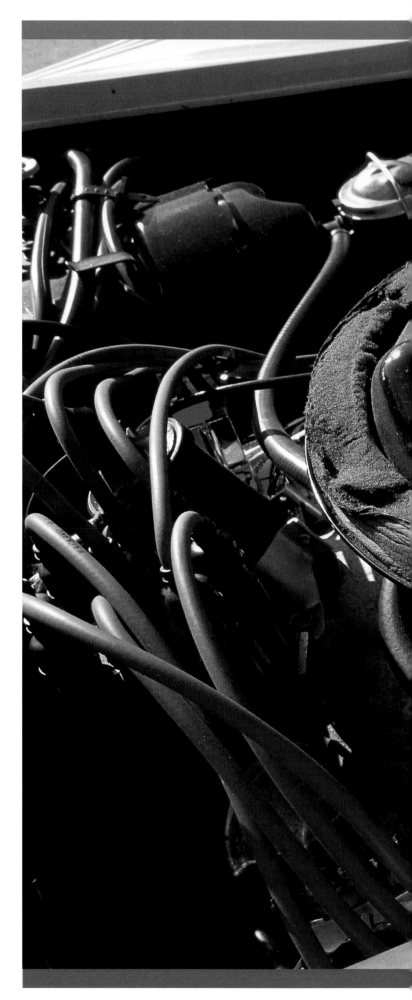

Even before the St. Louis production plant started its pre-assembly runs of the 1963 Sting Rays, Bill Mitchell told his designers to think about the next Corvette. The Sting Ray was to remain in production only through 1965, possibly carried over into 1966, so it was not too early to begin.

He set Larry Shinoda on a wild excursion with an open-wheeled single-seater like Arkus-Duntov's CERV I. It drew technical inspiration from Frank Winchell, Chevrolet Engineering Center's chief of R&D. Winchell had developed the production Corvairs and the Monza GT and SS prototypes in 1962 and 1963. Mitchell called his new car the X-15, named after the Air Force's black rocket plane. Shinoda worked with John Schinella and a small group of designers and modelers in another one of those invisible, locked studios. From it, Mitchell refined and defined what he wanted in his next personal car and in the next Corvette.

Previous Pages: *This aluminum L88, appropriately painted Daytona Yellow, represents an anomaly. Just two were built, and while one of them drag raced extensively, neither participated in road course events where the lighter engine weight would have aided handling as well as performance.*

Opposite: *With its hood up, the cowl induction system's plumbing comes into focus. The low-pressure area at the base of the windshield draws air into the rear of the hood, sucking it forward to the low-restriction air cleaner in the hood. The foam circle around the carburetor air intake seals the system.*

Shinoda's design, known internally as the XP-830, actually filled in at the last minute as a future Corvette when earlier plans failed. Arkus-Duntov's work on the CERV II had led to suggestions that the next-generation Corvette could be a mid-engined two-seater. Winchell's group had promoted the idea of a true lightweight (2,650-pound) rear-engined car, using the 327-ci V-8, but its rear weight bias made the car's handling a horror. Arkus-Duntov's concept was mid-engined, using the Mark IV 427, but the car had more neutral handling. Previous Corvettes had always been built out of parts produced for other Chevrolet models, but no pieces existed to build Arkus-Duntov's mid-engined two-seater. The costs to develop such pieces, even to a wealthy corporation such as GM, were prohibitive. Design exercises produced cars with shapes as striking as Lamborghini's mid-engine Miura. But while European exotic-car buyers might accept a price tag above $20,000, GM management was sure Corvette buyers would not. It was purely economic considerations, in combination with Donner's public indignation at the exploits of the Grand Sport and CERV I, that doomed the ambitious mid-engine next generation.

Engineering tried to make a Corvair chassis handle Corvette engines but, ultimately, found it impossible. The engineers and Mitchell's designers were facing an unforgiving timetable. In a forced-march pace, the two sides worked to bring a new car into existence.

Shinoda's creation for Mitchell became known as Mako Shark II. The earlier 1961 Shark show car, the XP-755, was renamed the Mako Shark I, to give consistency and longevity to styling exercises that would lead to the new car. The Mako II premiered at the New York International Auto Show in April 1965. By October, design was able to ship a running, functional model, powered by a Mark IV 427-ci V-8, to the Paris Salon. Throughout the rest of 1965, the two prototypes, which cost about $3 million to create, toured North America and Europe. They created a near frenzy of publicity and speculation. Magazines boldly printed that the Mako II was the basis for the next generation Corvette.

Above and opposite: *It is a deceptively subtle package at a time when manufacturers often emblazoned their "muscle cars" with wild, often outrageous graphics. This most potent of muscle cars, with more than 500 horsepower under the hood in stock trim, could easily be mistaken for Corvette's most popular 427-cubic-inch 390-horsepower package with the popular side-mounted exhausts.*

The RPO V54 luggage rack was designed to carry the T-top panels. Some 16,860 buyers paid $73 for the rack, which allowed them to make full use of the luggage area even when the tops were off.

Another variation available for 1978 was the Silver Anniversary model. This painted the car in light silver above and dark silver below a silver horizontal stripe. The option cost $399.

The Chevrolet studios worked to revise the Mako Shark II into something that could be produced for the public. The new body was built on the Sting Ray chassis, carrying over virtually everything mechanical from the production cars. By November 1965, Hank Haga's production studio produced full-size clay models close to what the finished car would look like. They replaced the Mako II boat-tail rear window with a scoop-like treatment derived from Arkus-Duntov's mid-engine prototype. When engineering tested these prototypes in their wind tunnel, however, Corvette's perpetual aerodynamic problems reappeared.

The new shark nose lifted even more than the Sting Ray's had. A duck-tail lip at the rear helped hold that end down, but it caused the nose to rise up farther. Arkus-Duntov fitted a small chin spoiler across the front, which helped somewhat.

Design retained the tall front fender bulges from the Mako Shark II show car, and again Arkus-Duntov found himself fighting Mitchell. Mitchell's preferences ran counter to engineering's practicality and driver visibility. Arkus-Duntov sought support from Pete Estes, Chevrolet's general manager. Estes disliked

Everyone knows Chevrolet did not build a convertible Corvette between model years 1976 and 1986, but if you wanted one, American Custom Industries had just the thing for you. It was even engineered by none other than Zora Arkus-Duntov. Even better, at Arkus-Duntov's insistence, it was turbocharged.

the sightlines over the wheel humps and sent the car back to the drawing boards.

Work was piling up in the engineering and design departments, which were already overburdened with the new Camaro, Chevrolet's response to Ford's Mustang and Pontiac's GTO. It was Chevy's entry into the muscle car wars, and this new car had to debut in 1967, as sales were lost to Pontiac and Ford daily. Everyone agreed to hold over the Sting Ray replacement until 1968.

Under supervision from Chevrolet chief stylist David Holls, Larry Shinoda worked with Haga and his staff to reduce the excesses of the Mako Shark II prototype. Mitchell had Haga's staff resurrect a removable roof panel idea that had appeared in the small experimental studios off and on since the late 1950s. The Corvette's fiberglass body and steel frame, however, were not stiff enough to accommodate an open roof. Incorporating a center beam that tied the windshield to the rear section, Chevrolet design adapted an innovation from industrial designer Gordon Buerhig: the T-roof.

CHAPTER SEVEN

Mitchell wanted the hidden headlights and windshield wipers of the Mako II on the production prototype, which caused new problems and delays. The retractable headlights, which had become part of the iconography of Corvette, partially obstructed the engine-cooling airstream when the headlights were closed. Developing the vacuum plumbing to operate lights and wiper covers powerful enough to punch through snow or ice took time. During late 1966 and early 1967, other problems had to be solved. Through the 1968 model year, engine cooling was barely sufficient for big-block engines with air-conditioning. Air-conditioning was a popular accessory, and inside the pinched cockpit, the newly introduced flow-through Astro-Ventilation system was completely inadequate.

These were the challenges that styling and engineering faced to get the Corvette completed for 1967. When Donner delayed the launch another year, it was a blessing to all.

Soon after introducing the 1968 model to the press, Chevrolet reorganized its division management, disbanding Corvette engineering. Arkus-Duntov was shuffled into special assignments; others, not so lucky, were reassigned to Chevrolet passenger car responsibilities.

Then the magazine reviews of regular production Corvettes began to appear. Most notable was a piece in *Car and Driver*. Editor Steve Smith wrote in the December 1967 issue about his plans to road test the 1968 Corvette he had just driven out to Watkins Glen. "But we won't," he wrote. "The car was unfit for a road test. No amount of envious gawking by the spectators could make up for the disappointment we felt at the car's shocking lack of quality control. With less than 2,000 miles on it, the Corvette was falling apart." With these few words, Smith succeeded in restoring a Corvette engineering department. Arkus-Duntov and his team were regrouped, and he was named chief engineer for the Corvette.

In an ironic twist, by year-end, *Car and Driver* readers voted the 1968 Corvette the "Best All-Around Car in the World."

The St. Louis factory had produced just three L88s in time for the 1968 Daytona 24 Hours endurance race. Actor James Garner bought them and prepped them in California. Those and two others not built in St. Louis but from over-the-counter engines installed by the racers all lost to a 1967 L88 coupe entered by Sunray DX. In February, Sunray got its first factory L88 hardtop. Don Yenko prepared that car and freshened up the other two put-together cars for Sebring. At the end of the race on March 23, Hap Sharp and Dave Morgan won the GT class in Sunray's factory-built L88, finishing sixth overall. Two Camaros and a Mustang finished ahead of them.

The Manta Ray

Bill Mitchell got restless once his Mako Shark II-based production model appeared in showrooms. Advanced design studio artists reinvented Mitchell's car, which he called the Manta Ray. By 1969, the elongated Mako

Above: *The new nose and tail pieces, first introduced with the 1980 production models, incorporated fully integrated spoilers. These reduced air drag considerably, improved mileage slightly, and increased radiator air flow by 50 percent.*

Right: *Exterior and interior colors respect the 1953 original, another homage to Corvette's history from ACI president Bob Schuller. But Schuller and Arkus-Duntov moved into the 80s with digital readout instruments, an in-dash computerized telephone and rear stowage cooler. In the end, ACI sold fewer than 100 of these cars*

Safety and Emissions Standards

As Chevrolet worked on developing its new Corvette model, lawmakers in Washington, D.C., and Sacramento, California, were working on developing new rules and regulations for emissions and safety standards for automobiles. As early as 1955 California was monitoring exhaust emissions, which inspired Arkus-Duntov to perfect a cleaner burning fuel-injected engine; the improved performance was serendipitous. For model year 1962, California required all new cars sold in the state to have positive crankcase ventilation (PCV) systems. By 1965, Congress was looking at legislation to formulate acceptable levels of auto-exhaust gas emissions. California mandated smog pumps on all 1966 models, and these same regulations went into effect nationwide with the 1968 model year. The Traffic Safety Act began setting front-, rear-, and side-impact and visibility standards for cars sold in the United States in 1966. It also established procedures requiring manufacturers to recall vehicles on which mechanical and safety flaws appeared. California introduced its own stricter auto-emissions standards, which became mandatory with 1969 models sold in that state.

The box-section steel tube frame swings low through the cockpit, making driver changes quick and easy. Ear protection was essential with the 850-horsepower engine exhaust exiting just below the doors through 4-inch pipes. Greenwood preparation was meticulous.

small-block, solid-lifter-equipped, LT1 350-ci engine. This engine came much closer to the preferences of Zora Arkus-Duntov, who had never favored the heavy big-block Mark IV engines that unbalanced the car. When Donner retired as GM's president and chairman, the board elected former Chevrolet chief Ed Cole—and performance was welcome again. Even the LT1, with its lighter weight but inferior output compared to the outrageous 427s, found a slot on an option list. The LT1 probably produced 370 horsepower, but like the earlier L88s, its output was down-rated to keep the increasingly safety-conscious public less mindful of Chevrolet's products.

At the other end of the spectrum, engine builders stretched the 427 Mark IV further, increasing it to 454-ci displacement. New designations appeared. The LS5 was a 454-ci engine with hydraulic valve-lifters that was rated at 390 horsepower. An all-aluminum LS7, conservatively rated at 460 horsepower and priced around $3,000, was listed but never offered. In racers' minds, an unrestrained LS7 would exceed 600 horsepower.

To address quality-control problems, every single Corvette was put through a water bath with an inspector riding inside looking for possible leaks. After that they ran the car over a two-mile road of exaggerated cobblestone and potholed surfaces, followed by a stint on a vibration table that flexed and torqued every car repeatedly. DeLorean allowed no failures to leave the plant.

Although Ed Cole remained a friend of performance, his perspective changed when he became chairman, as he was forced to confront broader issues. While the financial climate of the country was fairly healthy, with the gross national product up 7 percent and unemployment at a decade-low 3.5 percent, other concerns were challenging car companies in Detroit. Insurance rates for an unmarried 20-year-old male driving his own high-performance

Shark/Manta Ray was out on the show circuit, stopping viewers in their tracks, hinting at things to come from Mitchell's multimillion-dollar playground.

A two-month-long autoworkers strike created a backlog of public orders for the 1969 model, now named the Stingray as one word. New division general manager John DeLorean set back the new model introduction to February 1970, which partially explained the very high sales number for the 16-month 1969 model year. The corresponding eight-month 1970 season, however, recorded only 17,316 sales (10,668 coupes and 6,648 ragtops).

Chevrolet announced an engine option late in the 1969 model year, but it didn't appear until 1970. It was a

car reached $1,000 a year in 1968 and nearly $2,000 in 1970. Massachusetts introduced the country's first no-fault automobile insurance. On Earth Day, April 22, 1970, a nationally televised teach-in painted a grim picture of the world's environmental pollution, citing the automobile as the chief perpetrator.

Cole set out again to ensure the continued existence of the Corvette as he had done in the 1950s. He eliminated options with low sales volume and ordered engineers to rework all GM engines to run on low-lead 91-octane fuel. He told engineering, marketing, advertising, and public relations to use Society of Automotive Engineers (SAE) net measurement standards for engine horsepower output, numbers that were substantially lower than the gross-horsepower ratings previously published. The result was a slight improvement in auto insurers' regard for GM products.

Cole also wanted to keep racers as Chevy customers. Corvette introduced the ZR1 and ZR2 packages similar to the earlier Z06 options. No radio, power steering, power windows, or air-conditioning was available with either of these. The ZR2 used the LS6 454-ci 425 horsepower engine, and only twelve hardy racers bought one. The ZR1, based on the LT1, was an even rarer breed, with only eight buyers. Production car sales rose for 1971, totaling 14,680 coupes and 7,121 convertibles, 21,801 in all.

The real impact of the new clean-air standards was clear for the 1972 model year. Cole's cleanup had its effect as well; the LS6, which had sold only 188 copies in 1971, vanished. The only 454-ci engine left was re-rated down to 270 horsepower SAE, and 3,913 were sold. The solid-lifter LT1, listed at 255 horsepower, sold 1,741 copies, while the ZR1 package saw its last year on the options lists with only 20 delivered.

In all, Chevrolet sold 28,004 Corvettes in 1972, with 20,496 coupes delivered against 6,508 convertibles. It was a nice position for a new general manager to inherit, and that's what Jim McDonald found on October 1, 1972. Another Pontiac graduate, he knew the value of building a car in great demand. He increased production slightly, understanding the risks of too much inventory.

Back to Its Roots

As the car entered its 21st season, a pendulum began to swing back toward the Corvette's roots. New federal regulations required Corvette to forsake its recent high-performance identity if it was to survive.

For 1973, design revised the front fender side vents and eliminated the cowl flap that often left owners without working windshield wipers. The removable back window, carried over since its introduction in 1968, was also discontinued. Engineering fitted radial-ply tires, although the planned cast-aluminum lightweight wheels were never available due to quality problems. The 454-ci engine was carried over but revised to provide an additional 5 horsepower, now rated at 275 and renamed the LS4. The small-block, hydraulic-lifter L82 offered 250 horsepower from the 350-ci cast-iron engine. New body and engine mounts and additional sound insulation throughout the body stiffened the car and decreased road and mechanical noise.

Model year 1974 marked the end of high performance, which had been under attack for some time. In December 1970, Congress passed the Clean Air Bill in the National Environmental Policy Act, establishing regulations for fuel economy and emissions that the big blocks could never meet. Auto makers had less than six years to develop engines that would emit 90 percent less toxic gases. After 1974, there was no 454 and the small blocks lost true dual exhausts to a two-into-one pipe that ran through a catalytic converter before returning to dual-looking tailpipes.

An even worse shock was coming. In January 1971, members of an 11-year-old group called the Organization of Petroleum Exporting Countries (OPEC) failed to negotiate price increases with 17 western oil companies. The OPEC members agreed to set prices by themselves. Gas prices in the United States rose steadily. In mid-March 1974, OPEC, now 13 members strong, settled with its western customers, and crude oil that had sold for $2.11 per barrel in January 1971 went to $14.08 38 months later. Lines formed at gas stations and fuel economy suddenly made a difference. The White House ordered a nationwide 55 miles per hour "energy conservation" speed limit.

Despite all this, Chevrolet sold 30,460 Corvettes in 1973, 25,521 coupes and 4,943 convertibles, with many more buyers preferring the T-topped cars to convertibles. Barely a third purchased an optional engine, yet nearly two-thirds ordered the automatic transmission. The nature of Corvette buyers was changing and the car kept pace. The trend away from convertibles continued in 1974. Some 32,028 coupes sold versus only 5,474 ragtops. New production and sales records were set with 37,502 cars sold overall.

The Demise of the L82

On New Year's Day 1975, Zora Arkus-Duntov, Corvette's most devoted engineer and its chief engineer since December 1967, retired. He was replaced by Dave McLellan, a GM engineer since 1959. More personnel changes took place at the top. James McDonald moved out as general manager and was replaced in December 1974 by Robert Lund, who came from Cadillac. Model year 1975 marked the end of several other Corvette mainstays as well. Chevrolet no longer offered the L82 engine because of its excessive emissions. Convertible sales dwindled to only 4,629 cars, less than one-eighth of the total production of 38,469, so they were discontinued. In addition to production realities, outside pressures also pushed for the demise of the convertible Corvette. The federal government had been making noises about convertible roll-over safety as early as 1970, and congressional hearings and investigations led Detroit carmakers to expect a governmental mandate. Even though legislation never appeared, the economic considerations made it an easy decision for GM.

Corvette forged ahead through 1976 and 1977, producing two more record sales years and increasing prices. Engineers enhanced engine performance by improving air pumps and exhaust gas recirculation systems. Base power output returned to 180 horsepower, which was sufficient for

nearly 85 percent of the Corvette buyers in 1976 and 1977.

In mid-March 1977, Corvette reached a landmark when the 500,000th car came off the assembly line in St. Louis. This was a precursor to the facelift that appeared in 1978 to celebrate the 25th anniversary of the Corvette and the 62nd annual running of the Indianapolis 500.

To commemorate a quarter century of the car, dreamers behind locked doors in the design studios created mid-engine prototypes using small blocks, big blocks, and even multiple rotary engines clothed in fiberglass, thin sheet steel, and aluminum. Cold budgetary realities and differing opinions of what was a "true Corvette" doomed both the 25th anniversary and Indianapolis 500 commemorative cars to auto show stands.

For the public, quick and easy changes sufficed. Mitchell's sugar-scoop rear-window treatment was replaced with a large sloping back window. Under the hood, 1978 GM's Corporate Average Fleet Economy requirements limited the 350-ci L48 base engine to 185 horsepower (except in California, where emissions standards pulled another 10 horsepower from it). The optional L82 offered 220 horsepower. Total production reached 46,776 cars, including the B2Z optional Silver Anniversary and the replica Indy 500 Pace Car, one produced for each Chevrolet dealer.

The 1979 models gained in horsepower due to adoption of the twin-snorkel air cleaner from the L82, ingesting cooler outside air. This, plus adoption of the L82's lower back-pressure mufflers, gave the base L48 a 10 horsepower boost to 195 in all 50 states. The L82 also gained a 5 horsepower boost to 225. Thinner, lighter seats from the pace car became standard for all Corvettes in 1979. The Indy pace car spoilers were a $265 option for all Corvettes. Base price settled in at $10,220.23, and Chevrolet set yet another production record with 53,807 cars.

Corvette had been enormously profitable for several years now. Few people remained in the division who would buck the status quo. Arkus-Duntov left Chevrolet in January and Ed Cole soon followed, chased by Bill

Mitchell, who retired in 1978. Chevrolet's new director of engineering, Lloyd Reuss, had no desire to make waves. David McLellan, Arkus-Duntov's successor, resonated contentment and his preference for front-engined Corvettes.

In 1980, buyers got cars with a lower drag nose sporting a front chin spoiler. This aerodynamically friendly front end and the removal of 250 pounds of weight from the car were welcome improvements for the 1980 models. One change inside the car was not welcome, however. Federal standards that lowered national speed limits to 55 miles per hour required all speedometers to provide calibration no higher than 85 miles per hour, no matter what the car's actual top speed was. In California, only the base 305-ci engine would pass the state's stringent emissions requirements, so buyers there had to be content with this lower performance engine. Largely a result of numerous federal safety and emissions requirements, the suggested retail price for the base Corvette rose by nearly $3,000, to $13,140.24. Still, 40,614 buyers were undeterred and forked over the down payment or the first lease payment.

The improvements that followed in 1981 and 1982 were undramatic. The 49-state 350 was certified in California, but optional engines disappeared; 190 horsepower was all any buyer could get from the factory. Under the hood, a new Computer Command Control (CCC) module managed fuel and air mixture in the carburetor and ignition timing to produce optimum exhaust emission performance and fuel economy. This system first appeared in 1980 on California-only 350s.

Complaints continued from magazine reviews and buyers alike about the car's fit and finish. Quality control still seemed to be elusive for Chevrolet's most expensive and visible product. To address that problem, the company began producing its Corvettes at a new high-tech

Starting with the all-aluminum ZL1 L88 engine, Greenwood worked his magic, and rumors report he and Dick Smothers had better than 850 horsepower available. He and Smothers routinely saw 210 and 211 miles per hour on the Mulsanne Straight at Le Mans. Greenwood designed his own cross-ram magnesium intake manifolds.

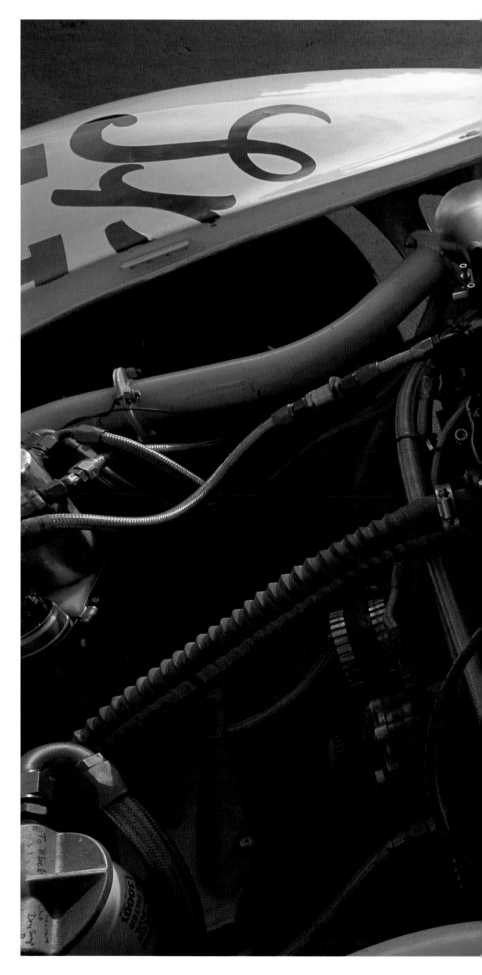

In typical Chevrolet understatement, this rarest-of-rare Corvettes sports the standard interior appointments. Except for a small badge near the gear shift that specified using the highest octane rating gasoline only for this aluminum block ZL-1, the rest of the interior could be found in any shopping center parking-lot variety small block. Only the plain panel where a radio belonged hinted that this car was something different from every other 1969 model.

assembly plant in Bowling Green, Kentucky, on June 1, 1981. Before GM acquired it, the plant had been Chrysler's air-temp division air-conditioner factory. Corvette assembly overlapped at the old St. Louis facility until model-year production ended on August 1. Bowling Green's new equipment offered not only tighter assembly standards but also new paint. Enamel base colors finished with clear topcoats came from Kentucky, while the remaining St. Louis cars were finished in lacquer.

Prices jumped another $3,100 as the car reached $16,258.52—about $1,660 more than Cadillac's El Dorado. The basic Corvette, however, was highly civilized, and the remaining options just made it cushier. Chevrolet sold 40,606 in all.

In 1982, Chevrolet introduced throttle-body fuel injection, which reappeared in a form called "Cross Fire Injection," and it bumped engine output to 200 horse-power. Engineering replaced the existing three-speed Turbo-Hydramatic with a new four-speed overdrive auto-matic transmission.

The final "Shark" was offered for 1982 as a well-equipped base model at $18,290.07, and also as a special-order Collector Edition. Product planners, who had seen the strong sales of the 25th anniversary model and the Indy Pace Car replica, called for a special exterior paint and interior trim option to honor the end of the longest production run and celebrate 30 years of Corvettes. Total production for 1982 was 25,407, anticlimactic after 15 years of production.

Still, in 15 years, Chevrolet sold more than half a million sharks, 542,861 in all, and that despite a limping national economy. As inflation kept up its relentless 10- to 13.5-percent rate, the prime rate shot up to 21 percent in 1980, making auto loans almost unaffordable at 24 percent. In 1981, GM announced its first loss since 1921, coming up $763 million short for the year. This forced the board to delay new projects or cancel them outright.

> In 1981, in the midst of a national recession, former Chevrolet general manager John DeLorean introduced his stainless-steel, mid-engined, Irish-built sports car, priced at $25,000. His knowledge of manufacturing steel-bodied automobiles outside the U.S. would do him no good, however, and his car would become a cult footnote once he was arrested for cocaine possession.

CORVETTE C4: WHERE ARE YOU?

CHAPTER EIGHT

CORVETTE C4: WHERE ARE YOU?

1983–1989

There was no 1983 Corvette. At least none that was intended for the public. Chevrolet assembled 70 "engineering" cars, and only one official survivor exists, on permanent display at the National Corvette Museum in Bowling Green, Kentucky. Historians can trace the decision to skip an entire production year as far back as 1977, when the Chevrolet division first imagined the next model, the fourth-generation Corvette.

Irwin Rybicki became GM's vice president of design after Bill Mitchell retired in 1977. Very different from Mitchell, Rybicki was a conservative, modest man who had directed the Buick-Oldsmobile-Cadillac studios through countless folded-edge designs that sold cars like mad. Rybicki inherited Mitchell's legacy and his staff. Jerry Palmer, who had done Corvette show cars for Mitchell in 1969, had been influencing the production cars since the 1973 model. In 1974, Mitchell named him chief designer of Chevrolet Studio 3, the home of the Corvette and Camaro, a job with high visibility and considerable influence.

Over in engineering, Dave McLellan was a veteran of similar training when he was Arkus-Duntov's protégé. McLellan found himself in a similar position to Palmer in being able to influence what

Previous pages and opposite: *The 1984 had the flattest-angle windshield to date at 64 degrees. The roof also divided into an openable hatchback—the largest compound surface glass formed until that time—and a removable glass roof panel over the seats. The 1984 model was introduced in March 1983, making it the first automobile that complied fully with federal emission and safety regulations. The new design provided higher ground clearance but lower overall height by moving the engine rearward and fitting exhaust and other plumbing into a wide center tunnel. Chevrolet produced 51,547 coupes, its best year since 1979.*

The large pad facing the passenger seat was part of a passive restraint system mandated by the federal government. It was nicknamed the "breadloaf."

any new Corvette would become. Palmer and McLellan learned that the GM board had decided to replace the long-running and highly profitable current-model Corvette, which at the time was generating more than $100 million annually. A totally new model was authorized for 1983 to celebrate the car's 30th anniversary. Because Palmer and McLellan had joined Chevrolet during the Mitchell/Arkus-Duntov Sting Ray era, this would be the first Corvette designed, developed, and sold without any link to Harley Earl and Ed Cole's 1953 model.

Ideas emerged quickly. Experiments with Wankel's rotary engines were disappointing, but engineering and design created the AeroVette with a transversely mounted 400-ci reciprocating V-8 that restored promise for a new

mid-engine configuration. GM had introduced Chevrolet's Citation X-11 and Pontiac's Phoenix, the X-body cars with transverse V-6 engines driving front axles. McLellan knew this technology was available, but Corvette's 205 horsepower was double what Citation/Phoenix 90- to 110- horsepower drive trains could handle. It meant instant failure or long, costly development work. At the same time, federal regulators proposed a gas-guzzler tax to punish fuel inefficiency. GM's fleet average for 1983 had to be 19 miles per gallon, no matter what performance the engineers developed for the Corvette. GM's board would never allow any of the company's cars to suffer that tax.

> **When John DeLorean was Chevrolet general manager he had proposed downsizing the Corvette onto the smaller Camaro/Firebird F-body platform, arguing that Corvette could share chassis and development expenses. Palmer and McLellan vigorously fought the idea, maintaining that DeLorean was more interested in increasing profits than improving the Corvette.**

Among the engineering and design staffs, the debates continued over front-engine versus mid-placement. Cast-iron big blocks skewed weight balance heavily to the front; mid-engine placement provided better handling but sacrificed load-carrying ability.

Heritage was on everyone's mind when McLellan and Palmer started their teams brainstorming and sketching ideas. Marketing worried that Corvette buyers would balk at anything that was radically different. The board, still smarting from the whole rear-engine Corvair adventure, had dragged its feet against Arkus-Duntov's campaign for a mid-engined Corvette. Despite Zora's objective of creating a sports car he could drive proudly in Europe, the Corvette was and always would be a car for American roads and drivers. And McLellan favored the traditional front-engine rear-drive Corvette, so that was that.

The C4 Arrives

When McLellan sought performance targets for the 1983 Corvette, everyone agreed they wanted the new model to be the best-handling sports car in the world. To him that dictated fat, low-profile tires on 10-inch-wide wheels. Since the time of the Grand Sports, Corvettes introduced the highest performance tires. McLellan accepted Arkus-Duntov's dictum that Corvette's suspension must remain compliant at full speed over uneven roads. This required vast suspension travel, but it ensured that no driver would be thrown out of control at top speed because the suspension bottomed out.

Design chief Jerry Palmer wanted 16-inch wheels for styling purposes. When McLellan's engineers set the first specifications on paper, they established minimum ground clearance at 5.25 inches, up a quarter inch from the C3 third-generation Corvette. They placed four squat tires at the corners, and the car's design began from there, capitalizing on GM's relationship with Goodyear Tire & Rubber. Engineering wanted tires capable of 140- to 145-mile-per-hour speeds. They also demanded crisp handling, a quiet ride, efficient water shedding, an interesting appearance, and a minimum 10,000-mile tread life even with enthusiastic use. Goodyear based its efforts on its Formula One rain tire development and produced the VR50 "Gatorback," which met Corvette's parameters with room to spare.

Room to spare was what the tires missed. Fat front tires needed space to clear engine and suspension pieces under full-lock turning. Fitting the Gatorbacks inside the bodywork necessitated widening the car by 2 inches, and McLellan had to settle for 8.5-inch tires because the 10-inchers stuck out beyond the new body.

Owner surveys indicated that the Corvette's Coke-bottle shape pinched shoulder room and created a claustrophobic cockpit. Widening the car helped remedy that, but there were other concerns, too. Safety, styling, and engineering improvements over 25 years had added weight and

increased size; GM's board now ordered divisions to downsize each vehicle. The Corvette design team filled in the long-standing pinched waist, thus adding 6.5 inches to interior shoulder room.

McLellan's engineers widened the center tunnel enough to feed the driveshaft, exhaust, catalytic converter, plumbing, and wiring between the seats now instead of below them. Maintaining their minimum ground clearance, they still lowered the seating floor 2 inches to the bottom of the chassis. This increased headroom yet lowered the roofline an inch. In turn, this reduced frontal area, decreasing aerodynamic drag and improving fuel economy. With a more efficient packaging of the mechanical necessities, McLellan and Palmer shortened overall length by 8.4 inches from the existing model. It was wider, yes, but it was also lower, shorter, and more fuel-efficient.

By early spring 1979, McLellan's engineering staff had a few development mules out testing. Palmer's Studio 3 design staff began creating the new car's look. Randy Wittine, called "Mr. Corvette" because of his 15 years of involvement with the car, worked alongside a new kid on the block, John Cafaro. Cafaro, the studio's youngest designer since Peter Brock, produced a rendering of the new car that incorporated a hood that revealed the engine,

While Dick Guldstrand drove this one only briefly, the California influence extended not only to the Showroom Stock racing series but to the car itself. Its superb rear suspension was developed from existing successful Guldstrand Corvette racer.

front tires, suspension, and chassis. The hood opened like a clamshell, split along a seam that ran horizontally around the entire car. In this one drawing, Cafaro created two signature styling features. With the tilt front-end, Palmer saw an opportunity to make the engine and mechanical parts appear integrated. McLellan agreed, and both staffs coordinated engine castings, forged suspension pieces, and even spark plug wires for appearance as well as function, and they color coordinated pieces to add visual impact. Cafaro's clamshell seam simplified both molding and joining the fiberglass body panels. His design began to make possible tighter quality control in fit and finish.

Roger Hughet, Palmer's chief assistant, worked with Charles Toner and his aerodynamics engineers to improve the body shape in wind tunnels at speeds up to 140 miles per hour. These tests confirmed that Cafaro's chin spoiler shoveled up enough ground-level air to reach the radiator behind his grille-less front end. The high-speed wind tunnel experiments led to the reintroduction of fender-side "gills," the air extractor slots that vented air-pressure

Sports Car Club of America rules for the Showroom Stock Grand Touring class required a full roll cage and fire-suppression systems in the cockpit. Otherwise the interior had to remain as it came from the dealer.

buildup—the same pressure that popped hoods on Arkus-Duntov's Grand Sports at speed.

As early as 1978, Palmer's interior designers began to mate the instrument panel and seating to the sleek new exterior. They had federal regulations to worry about, including Motor Vehicle Safety Standard 208, for driver and passenger safety in a front-end collision. The driver had the collapsible steering column in the event of a head-on crash; the passenger got a padded structure nicknamed the "breadloaf" because of its looks.

Congress introduced Motor Vehicle Safety Standard 208 in 1977 to go into effect for model year 1982. It became a political issue and was postponed for 1985 introduction. In October 1981, President Reagan revoked it altogether, but it was too late for designers to scrap it. The breadloaf was part of the Corvette, located where the glove box should be.

Chevrolet carried over the throttle-body, cross-ram induction V-8 introduced with the 1982 Shark, adding improvements to engine management, a serpentine belt accessory drive, and an electric cooling fan in front of the radiator. It looked perfect under Cafaro's hood.

McLellan's engineers mated the engine to their innovative 4+3-speed manual transmission, a clever variation on the standard Warner Division gearbox re-engineered by Doug Nash. Coupled to the Delco Electronic Control Module (ECM), the Nash transmission provided what were essentially short shifts in second, third, and fourth gears. It was like an automatic manual transmission, configured specifically to improve mileage for the EPA test. Engineering replaced the earlier heavy iron Delco-Moraine disc brakes with Australian Repco aluminum-and-iron versions, saving 70 pounds between the four brakes.

McLellan's people improved the suspension as well, setting out to achieve 1.0g of lateral-acceleration cornering power. Their chassis innovations, suspension configuration changes, and Goodyear's Gatorback tires made it possible.

Engineering constructed the chassis from thin sheets of high-strength, low-alloy (HSLA) steel, spot welded into boxes and other shapes to support front and rear suspension, engine, differential, roof, doors, and windshield. Previous Corvette frames involved two separate elements, one chassis/frame and the other a "birdcage" of much smaller members fitted above the chassis/frame to support the body. With the new car, the fiberglass surface panels merely hid the frame and running gear. Past ladder frames had required cross-members in order to tie outer frame rails together and add structural rigidity to the car, but engineers accomplished this with a single bolted-in cross-member used as a front-engine support. Though the entire frame weighed just 351 pounds, it was rigid enough to allow a completely removable roof center section that no longer required the T-roof support.

Suspension engineers hung all-aluminum forged suspension pieces on this chassis. The independent rear suspension used a five-link system instead of the previous model's three links, which fixed the rear axle more positively in place, eliminating its tendency to steer the car from the back in certain suspension load-unload transitions. They mounted fiberglass leaf springs transversely

It wasn't an outright champion in 1985, but Kim Baker's racer won the SSGT crown in 1986 and 1987. Chevrolet provided enormous technical assistance, but some of his most generous help came from Goodyear Tire & Rubber.

If speed gets your attention, than this car should grab you. August 2001: 223.051 miles per hour on the salt flats at Bonneville, Utah. It took Ed and Linda Van Scoy four years to crack the 220 miles per hour barrier.

When Corvettes proved indomitable, the SCCA catered to other competitor manufacturers and outlawed the cars. Quickly, Canadian racer John Powell and others created a plan to run a one-marque series, the Corvette Challenge.

on the front and rear suspensions. Fiberglass was lighter, more resilient, and wouldn't sag after millions of jounce and rebound cycles. Engineers also had the transverse springs do double-duty as anti-sway bars, and it worked so well that the diameter of the supplemental anti-sway bar was greatly decreased.

McLellan's engineers raced against time and their desire to get everything right. Magazines told consumers

a completely new Corvette was coming, and sales of the 1982 model fell off so dramatically that they began dismantling the production line at Bowling Green in anticipation of the model changeover.

GM's board faced a dilemma: engineering hadn't finished with the car. Should they release a car that was not ready for production? Two other factors influenced the verdict. If GM waited until early spring, it ensured that Chevrolet had the first 1984 model available, rather than the last 1983. It also meant Chevrolet would introduce the first automobile that met 1984 emissions and barrier-impact standards. The board slowed engineers enough to

conquer the 1984 regulations completely, and thereby avoid the need to re-engineer a hastily completed car. Production fired up on January 3, 1983, and each of the cars bore a vehicle identification number (VIN) identifying it as a 1984 car. (There are reports that 11 cars appeared with 1983 VIN numbers as well.)

Consequently, the 1984 model year was 17 months long, and when it was over and GM completed count, 51,547 buyers drove Corvettes home. Two years after its introduction, Chevrolet's chief engineer Don Runkle spoke with *Road & Track's* John Lamm about the 1984 and 1985 cars.

"We more or less moved the Corvette away from the classic Corvette customer," Runkle said. "It was deliberate on our part, primarily because we wanted to make a technical statement with it, but we couldn't figure out how to keep it where it was price-wise and also make that statement.

"We didn't have to make the car cost as much as it does. But if we hadn't put all those features (aluminum front suspension arms, plastic springs, tuned port injection, etc.) into it, the car wouldn't be as good as it is right now . . . I don't hear many people making fun of the Corvette anymore."

For the 1985 cars, Corvette engineers addressed complaints about ride harshness, adjusting shock valving on

CHAPTER EIGHT

No engine modifications were permitted except for removing the catalytic converters to prevent overheating. The cars were otherwise street legal. The engines, matched as closely as possible, were sealed at the Flint engine plant.

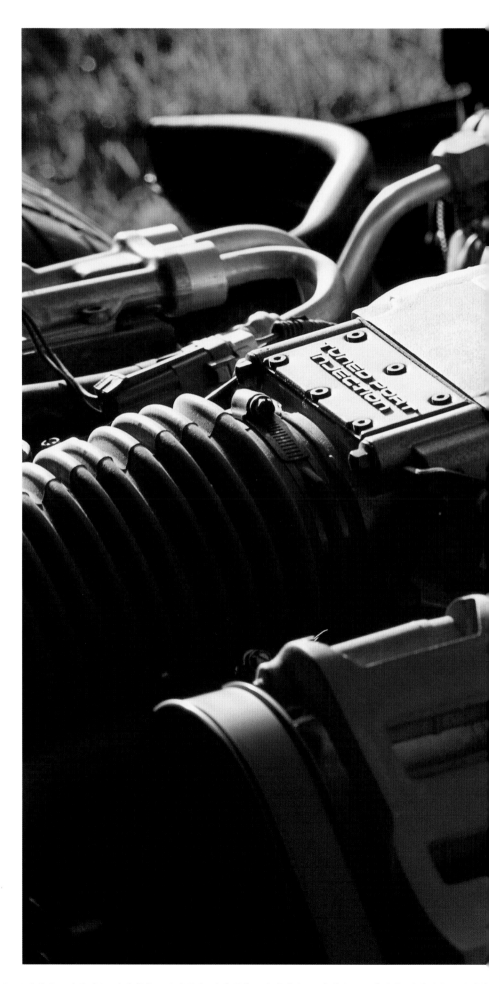

both the base shocks and the Z-51 Bilstein gas shocks and spring rates in the fiberglass transverse leaves. The rear wheels grew to 9.5-inch widths during the 1984 production run; the fronts were upsized for 1985.

Under the hood, Chevrolet continued to meet EPA numbers while improving performance. Tuned Port Injection replaced Cross Fire Throttle Body injection. The result was engine output up to 230 horsepower, a 0–60 mile per hour time of 6.6 seconds, and top speed nearer the magic 150 miles per hour. The second year of C4 was a 12-month sales year, and the total reflected more accurately the continuing interest in the car. In all, 39,729 cars were sold.

A convertible Corvette arrived near the middle of the 1986 model year. Although the chassis easily accommodated the "Targa" type removable roof, the open car required substantial reinforcement. Engineers enlarged the bolt-in cross-member ahead of the engine and the braces connecting that piece to the frame rails. They also fitted a large X-brace below the passenger compartment and added two more crosspieces behind the seats. Convertible buyers could not get the stiff Z51 suspension, but the 9.5-inch wheels were part of the convertible's own dedicated Z52 suspension. Chevrolet introduced the ragtop in bright yellow Indianapolis Pace Car replica trim. Base price for the convertible was $32,507, while the base coupes retailed at $28,502. One new standard item was an intelligent ignition key with an identification sensor, part of an overall Vehicle Anti-Theft System (VATS). Any key inserted into the ignition other than the one coded to the car would fail to start, disabling the ignition for three minutes.

Performance improved once again, with Z51-equipped coupes turning 0–60 in 5.8 seconds and registering top speeds of 154 miles per hour. The convertibles were good

Chevrolet built 60 Challenge racers, though only 30 of them ever saw competition.

for nearly 140 miles per hour with the top down. Chevrolet produced 7,315 convertibles and 27,794 coupes for the 1986 model year.

Engineering boosted the engine another 10 horsepower to 240 for 1987 with roller-bearing hydraulic valve-lifters that lessened friction, among other changes. They also redesigned the heads to improve burn efficiency by centering the spark plugs in the combustion chamber. Engineering fitted the same stiffening measures used on 1986 convertibles to the 1987 coupes. Chevrolet continued to offer the Z51 suspension on the coupe (with manual transmissions), and the convertible carried over its own Z52 version. Bearing a $33,647 base price, convertible sales increased to 10,625. Coupes slipped to 20,007, making for a total of 30,632 cars sold, down nearly 5,000 from the previous year.

The slotted wheels on the 1988 Corvette were nicknamed "Cuisinart" wheels because they looked like the food processor's blades.

For 1988, engineers provided a new less-restrictive exhaust system, good for an increase of 5 horsepower, taking the performance axle–equipped engine to 245 horsepower. They fitted lower profile Goodyear Z-rated P255/50ZR-16 tires (to allow speeds above 149 miles per hour) on 16-inch wheels. An optional Z51 (coupes only) and Z52 Performance Handling Package offered 12-slot, 17- by 9.5-inch wheels with Goodyear 275/40ZR-17 tires. The front disc brakes were changed to dual-piston versions that wrapped around thicker rotors for more braking

power and better brake cooling. Rear-suspension rebound travel was increased and front-suspension geometry was reconfigured to improve directional control in severe braking conditions.

Because 1988 marked the car's 35th anniversary, design and product planners created a commemorative edition of 2,000 white coupes with a white leather interior. Production dipped in 1988 despite the car's measurable improvements, with Chevrolet selling only 7,407 convertibles and 15,382 coupes, for a total of 22,789 cars. The coupe base price was up to $29,955, while the convertible sat at $35,295.

Chevrolet had scheduled the much-anticipated ZR1 for 1989 release, but it wasn't quite ready, so they introduced two elements of the long-rumored car. One was a six-speed manual transmission operated by its own computer, the Computer-Aided Gear Selection (CAGS)—another effort to satisfy both the EPA and the performance lover. When accelerating at one-third throttle or less at speeds below 20 miles per hour with a fully warmed engine, the CAGS blocked the gates to second and third gear so the shift went straight from first to fourth. At 20 miles per hour in fourth, the engine idled along at 1,050 rpm. Though the system earned little respect among enthusiasts, it did make very clear the quality and quantity of torque that the 350-ci L98 engine produced. While cruising at 65 miles per hour in sixth gear, the engine loafed at barely 1,600 rpm. Buyers who ordered the six-speed gearbox also got an engine oil cooler, heavy-duty radiator, and electric radiator cooling fan that were part of the Z51 package.

The other feature Corvette introduced for 1989 was the FX3 Selective Ride Control Delco-Bilstein electronic suspension. Chevrolet offered this only on Z51-equipped six-speed coupes. Drivers could change the four gas-filled Bilstein shock absorbers by a cockpit control that adjusted shock valving from "Touring" or "Sport" to "Per-

formance" settings that also varied within each shock based on the car's speed at the moment.

The wheels also now contained tire air-pressure monitors that transmitted signals to the instrument panel if pressure fell below desired levels. This system was intended for 1988 introduction, but last-minute problems delayed it to 1989. Base Corvette price including the Z52 suspension/handling package was $32,045 for the coupe. Sales reached 26,412 coupes and rose again to 9,749 ragtops.

The Corvette Challenge

With the new C4, the Corvette factory openly helped teams like Morrison Motorsports, Bakeracing, Rippie Racing, and Powell Motorsports further the development of their racing cars, which in turn fed back to the factory important wear and durability information about the chassis, drive train, and tires. Racetracks became two-way streets for information and cooperation, benefiting engineers, drivers, and enthusiasts.

"Even though Corvettes were able to beat every car that challenged them in the SCCA's Showroom Stock series," wrote Gregory von Dare in his book *Corvette Racers*, "they still had to race each other. That's where the fun started."

The "fun" began outside Parkman, Ohio, at an old racetrack called Nelson Ledges, only 100 miles from Detroit. In 1979, the track staged its first 24-hour endurance race for showroom stock cars. It drew only 19 entries but much interest. Each year the entry list grew, and when Chevrolet brought out its new Camaro and Porsche had its first 944 in 1983, the organizers found they had to create a "prototype" class. Porsche's front suspensions proved too fragile for Nelson's city street-like surface. Then the new Corvettes arrived in 1984 and stunned the racing world by winning 19 races in 19 starts. For four years straight, Corvettes took every race in the series run first as the Playboy Challenge, then as SCCA Showroom Stock

Grand Touring, and finally as the Escort GT Endurance series. Drivers in lesser cars recalled nursing their ailing entries into corners in the rain, watching a Corvette storm past them implausibly fast, its driver adjusting the radio or the heater, then using the ABS brakes to haul the car through the turn. Kim Baker, owner and co-driver of the yellow #4 Bakeracing Corvette, won the series in 1985 and 1986. At the end of 1987, Porsche and others hinted that they might withdraw if the SCCA didn't level the field. The SCCA banned Corvettes from its series beginning in 1988, but Corvette racers were not done.

Canadian racer John Powell reacted quickly. Gathering the support of Baker, Morrison, and others, he proposed to the SCCA a single-marque series, a Corvette Challenge, based on barely modified production cars. The SCCA challenged him to make it work, and Powell quickly got the support of Corvette development manager Doug Robinson. Then he enlisted major sponsorship from parts supplier Mid-America Designs and its enthusiast owner Mike Yager, from Goodyear Tire & Rubber, and from Exxon. Chevrolet's general manager Robert Berger approved lending the car's name to the series but made it clear that GM had no money to fund it.

Within a matter of months, Powell had pulled together the Million Dollar Corvette Challenge series, and the SCCA put 10 one-hour race dates on the calendar beginning May 1, 1988, at the Grand Prix of Dallas. Powell promoted the series well enough to entice some of the sport's leading drivers, including Jeff Andretti, Bobby and Tommy Archer, Kim Baker, John Greenwood, Tommy Kendall, Scott Legase, Johnny Rutherford, Jimmy Vasser, and Desire Wilson. Chevrolet produced 56 matching C4s, removing catalytic converters but otherwise remaining completely stock. Nine buyers never raced or converted their cars. For the rest, Powell lined up ProtoFab Engi-

neering to add roll cages, on-board fire-extinguishing systems, racing seats, and Bilstein shocks. Racers drove the break-in miles on the way from Detroit to their own shops. Racers paid their dealers for the cars, then an additional $15,000 to Powell for ProtoFab's conversion and their 1988 season entry fee.

By midyear, the series was in serious trouble, coming up about half a million dollars shy of its target. Powell went back to Chevrolet and appealed to Mike Goodman, the division marketing manager. Goodman sensed that this series was selling cars, and so he found the funds and signed a deal to continue the series through 1989. With that assurance, ESPN agreed to broadcast every Challenge race during the second year.

Graphics on the 1988 cars were subtle and the muffled exhausts too quiet to attract attention. The series and the SCCA modified the rules for 1989 by allowing entrants to get their own sponsorships, which enhanced each car's visual appeal considerably. Engineering changed the exhausts so spectators could hear the cars coming and going. Chevrolet constructed 61 of the racers for 1989, although perhaps as many as 31 never got converted to racers.

The races provided great drama, with entrants often qualifying within hundredths of seconds of each other. ESPN's coverage put viewers inside the cars with full-functioning gauge-readouts on screen. Chevrolet authorized assembly for 1990 even as regular production sales increased through 1989, validating Goodman's suspicions. Chevy manufactured just 23 cars, coded R9G, before pulling the plug on its sponsorship.

Meanwhile, the rest of the racing world had grown envious of the ESPN coverage and had caught up with Corvette's innovative chassis and ABS brakes. The SCCA invited Corvette back into its general series for 1990.

KING OF THE HILL

CHAPTER NINE

THE KING OF THE HILL

1990–1996

The very nature of Chevrolet's sports car has always been an unresolved issue. From Harley Earl's dream to Ed Cole's tool to Zora Arkus-Duntov's race car, the Corvette has meant something different to each creator. From the beginning up through the two-seat personal luxury car that Dave McLellan and Jerry Palmer created, the decision makers have molded and directed the Corvette. The goal has always been a vehicle they hoped each board chairman, from Alfred Sloan through Roger Smith, would bless with a production future.

In early 1986, Chevrolet chief engineer Don Runkle talked with *Road & Track* editors about the future of Corvette. He described what the car would become in later years. "We could obviously build a $100,000 Corvette and blow away the [Ferrari] Testarossa," Runkle said, "but I'm not sure what the point of that exercise is. That just shows that you can do it. Our goal is to do it at 25 percent of the price."

Runkle described a project involving engineering expertise from Lotus and Chevrolet, an engine producing perhaps 400 brake horsepower. This was the car that resurrected the Arkus-Duntov code name ZR1 and brought it to a much wider audience. It made Chevrolet division a lot of money, and it definitely reiterated the high-tech nature of the car.

"It is so expensive," Runkle said at the time. "Some people at Chevrolet don't think the additional volume it would generate would be worth the investment. My position is that this project has nothing to do with volume. This is to get the Corvette to be an unquestioned leader."

Within weeks, Runkle's prediction moved toward reality. At about 2:30 on the morning of May 1, 1986, engineers at Lotus in Norwich, England, fired up the first LT5, Chevrolet's brand-new dual-overhead camshaft, four valves-per-cylinder, small-block V-8. They ran it up to 3,000 rpm and held it for 30 minutes. Then they shut it off and uncorked champagne.

The LT5 was Chevrolet's first new V-8 since the Mark IV in 1965. Getting it done required some unusual alliances, the recognition of values beyond costs, and the

Previous pages: *There were numerous arguments about how the car should appear. Subtlety won out and only a minor enlargement of the rear bodywork, square taillights, and understated badging marked the car for what it was.*

Right: *The most obvious difference between regular production models and the ZR1 was the wider rear end (with square tail-lamp lenses). It was enlarged to accommodate Goodyear's P315/35ZR17 rear tires and 11-inch-wide wheels.*

Since the ZR1s reappeared as press prototypes in 1989, racers like Tommy Morrison wondered how they would hold up as racers. At the end of the 1991 Daytona 24 Hours he knew, with one finishing 12th overall and this one coming in 21st.

identification of who Corvette's next generation of competitors would be and what they would do.

Russ Gee, a director of powertrain engineering at Chevrolet-Pontiac-Canada (CPC), continued alternate powerplant research for the Corvette. Inside Chevrolet and out, engineers knew that the Corvette's engine was its only shortcoming. They had steadily improved the small-block V-8 since its introduction in 1955. Gee tried turbocharging V-6 engines, reconsidering mid-engine installations. He encountered critical vibration problems and fatal philosophical ones: Corvette owners perceived any engine with fewer than eight cylinders as un-Corvette-like. Early experiments with turbocharging Chevy V-8 engines yielded unacceptable fuel economy (though Reeves Callaway later worked through those).

As chief engineer, Lloyd Reuss had overseen the Cosworth four-valve head development for the Vega. He wondered about the V-8. Russ Gee began work in October 1984. In November, Tony Rudd, managing director of Lotus (owned by GM at this time), offered his firm's engineering services. Runkle, Reuss, Gee, and Rudd made a plan to create four-valve, dual-overhead camshaft heads to fit Chevrolet's small block. Rather than developing new heads, engineers and project managers concluded it made more sense to create an entirely new engine.

Reuss went to GM chairman Roger Smith and presented the benefits that this engineering offered, over time, to other products throughout GM's entire line, and he emphasized the Japanese threat. The Corvette was significant in Japan because it was the Japanese car manufacturers' target, and Smith agreed with that. Engineering designated the project the LT5; Runkle called it the King of the Hill.

Electrical problems and a major impact with another racer slowed the overall progress of this ZR1. The carbon-fiber bodywork saved nearly 600 pounds. Its teammate, car #92, is on permanent display at the Smithsonian Institution in Washington, D.C.

The improved ZR1 Corvette attracted attention from German and Japanese car builders who believed they could build one even better. Porsche had used the car as its benchmark for engineering the 944, and if SCCA's Showroom Stock racing series was any indication, Porsche gained respect for Corvette's engineers. Nissan engineers who produced the legendary Z-cars used Corvettes as CAD-CAM computer screensavers. Honda made it clear they produced their high-tech, mid-engined Acura NSX to show how much technology Japanese engineers had learned from America's automakers.

Dave McLellan studied the performance characteristics of every exotic car that Corvette owners might consider if they won the lottery. He concluded that the LT5 must get the Corvette to 60 miles per hour in four to five seconds. He knew that required at least 360 horsepower, but 400 had a better ring to it. It could not be a gas guzzler. They would design it from scratch, adopting no parts

from any existing GM engine. Then came the tough part: McLellan wanted a prototype engine running by May 1986 and one in a car three months later. It was made clear to Lotus that this engine, which might only have a total production run of 6,000 units, would be treated the same as any engine GM expected to go into six million automobiles, subject to every test, analysis, and second-guess.

Once Smith approved the LT5, Chevrolet had to find a plant in which to manufacture it. It was too small a run for any GM facility, which meant outside vendors. Roy Midgley selected Mercury Marine in Stillwater, Oklahoma. Mercury's sophisticated computer-controlled manufacturing technology could engineer aluminum castings. After months of meetings, Mercury learned in mid-March 1986 that it was to be the engine's builder.

Around this same time in 1986, Lotus began gathering parts from suppliers throughout Europe and the United States to build the prototype engine. Jerry Palmer's staff in Chevrolet Studio 3 made sure that, if owners raised John Cafaro's large hood, they saw an engine that looked like 400 horsepower. Some features had to be obvious. Lotus engineers concluded that dual-injection intake ports per cylinder were the best way to ensure optimum fuel mix for performance and economy. On partial throttle below 3,000 rpm, each cylinder used one inlet runner, one injector, and one inlet valve. The cam lobe for that valve provided mild timing with little overlap. A heavier foot signaled the electronic control module (ECM) to open the butterflies in the second runners and turn on their injectors. Cam timing for the second intake valves was wilder. Palmer's designers created 16 distinct tubes running from the injection system's main plenum to the cylinders below. They outlined the dual overhead camshafts in sculpted cam covers. The result was an industrial designer's dream: function dictated form that resulted in something beautiful to see.

By early 1987, Lotus ran brutal durability tests on the development engines. One trial ran alternately at peak horsepower speed for five minutes and then at peak torque speed for five minutes continuously for 200 hours. Cracks appeared in the cast crankshaft that forced an expensive specification change to nitrided forged steel. From there on, the LT5 tested flawlessly. On Christmas Eve 1987, Mercury Marine ran the first preproduction prototype LT5 on their dynamometer.

Lotus prepared to assemble an engine with production parts starting in January 1988. Since there was still testing to do, the LT5 would never make a September 1988 introduction. Reuss and Runkle wanted to provide a warranty that demanded they have it right. If the engine broke, GM would replace it; that kind of reliability required some 2,000 design changes. They balanced every moving part within the engine to tolerances common to Formula One racing engines capable of 14,000 rpm—far beyond the LT5's 7,000.

At a press demonstration, Terry Stinson, the LT5 project engineer at Mercury Marine, balanced a nickel on its edge on the engine plenum in a completed running car. It remained there, on edge, until he retrieved it.

Handling and Holding the Road

When McLellan compared his vision of the new Corvette to the competition, he recognized that the car needed not only exceptional power but also extraordinary handling and road holding. Prior to being purchased by GM, Lotus had startled the Formula One world with its active suspension system. The system used hydraulic pumps and cylinders, and sometimes the system did not keep up with the speed of the car, causing unsettling changes. Once it was outlawed, Lotus set it aside.

Active suspension next appeared in Porsche's 959, shown in racing trim as early as 1984 and as a $200,000+ road car in 1986. The electronic system, developed with assistance from Bosch, performed flawlessly. Active suspension intrigued McLellan and others when it was Lotus' project and later when it appeared on a Chevrolet-sponsored racer in the International Motor Sports Association (IMSA) series.

In the early 1980s, rumors circulated that NASCAR would change engine regulations to require V-6s rather than V-8s by the middle of the decade. Indianapolis engine wizard Ryan Falconer worked on Chevy V-6s and routinely pulled nearly 1,200 horsepower from turbocharged versions. That caught the attention of NASCAR team owner Rick Hendrick, who looked for another racing series in which to hide his own development efforts. Back in 1980, IMSA had created a grand touring prototype (GTP) class to encourage European teams to compete in their modified 250-miles-per-hour Group C cars on American circuits. Chevrolet let Hendrick know in late 1985 that it would support his effort, and Hendrick hired IMSA GTP veteran Ken Howes to run it. Howes believed that while Lotus' suspension system was troublesome in ultralight F1 cars, the greater room and weight allowance of a GTP car offered the system great potential. As the effort came together, Corvette designer Randy Wittine sketched the body that became the Corvette GTP.

The car first raced in August 1985 at Road America in Wisconsin, with about 800 horsepower in a chassis built for Chevrolet by England's Eric Broadley. The Lotus active suspension used dozens of sensors to register road surface traction and chassis dynamics. It flexed the suspension to eliminate body roll on cornering, rear squat on acceleration, and nosedive on braking. This kept the tires flat on the roadway without transferring unwanted dynamics back to the passenger compartment.

The car was spectacularly fast, qualifying on the pole for dozens of events between mid-1985 and the end of the program in late 1988. Corvette GTPs won outright at West Palm Beach, Florida, and at Road Atlanta. The highly stressed V-6 failed sometimes and the suspension challenged engineers, but Chevrolet continued its support because the engines offered promise for Camaro production models and the suspension offered what Dave McLellan envisioned for the Corvette ZR1. He built at least one prototype with the GTP system. It fit crab-like over the LT5 engine, its plumbing adding 200 pounds to the car, about 6 inches to the hood height, and immeasurable uncertainty to the reliability of the car. The GTP proved that active suspension was worth the effort. McLellan sent his engineers to work with Bosch on a modified version of Porsche's electronic system.

Introducing the LT5

The worldwide introduction of the LT5 took place in Geneva, Switzerland, in March 1989. Journalists raced the cars through mountains and praised the crews at Lotus, Mercury Marine, and Corvette. A few months earlier, in September 1988, the LT5 was revealed to the media during a press launch at Riverside Raceway. When fired up for a demonstration, the new engine was greeted very enthusiastically by those in attendance.

The first production engines built by Mercury employees came off the line on July 13, 1989. The engines developed 380 horsepower and the new Corvettes reached 60 miles per hour in 4.2 seconds and a top speed of 172 miles per hour. They met McLellan's target.

Roy Midgley and his crew worked to get still more power. Subtly modifying and improving air intakes, revising cam timing, and reducing exhaust back pressure helped them reach 405 horsepower by 1993. Even more impressively, they cleared the EPA gas-guzzler mark of 22.5 miles per gallon. With 405 horsepower and 180-mile-per-hour capability, it returned 23.1 miles per gallon on the test cycle.

A car running 170 to 180 miles per hour needed powerful brakes to haul down this 3,000-pound-plus missile. In early days of development before engines were ready, development mules were still narrow-body Corvettes, not wide versions needed to accommodate Goodyear's new tires. Engineering built a 400-horse-power V-8 with nitrous-oxide injection added to it. This would get the car to its top speed in the least distance to allow more runoff in case the brakes failed. Chevrolet hired Corvette Challenge racers Kim Baker and John Powell to do handling and brake testing. In Powell's first test, he targeted a 0.5g deceleration test from maximum speed to get a feel for the car. The calibration was incorrect, however. When Powell got on the brakes, he

Chevrolet provided 87 of these Pace Car replica convertibles to the Indy Speedway for festival and promotional uses. They also produced another 415, one for each of Chevy's top dealers.

brought the car to a standstill at nearly 1.0g without any problem.

One troubling question Chevrolet faced was whether it should adorn the body with wings, spoilers, or scoops. Reuss wanted visual significance; Palmer disagreed, preferring subtle differences from previous models. Palmer's staff mocked up Reuss' ideas, eventually incorporating many of them in the entire Corvette lineup for 1991. Only Palmer's understated widening of the car's rear end and its squarish taillights distinguished the LT5. The back-end enlargement, 1.5 inches on each side, started with new outer door panels feathering in the additional size. It accommodated Goodyear's first 35-series Eagle road tire, P315/35ZR-17 rears, mounted on 11-inch-wide wheels.

The final question was a name. "King of the Hill" was what it had become, but many insiders knew this would provoke challengers to try to depose the king. There were other considerations, too. For the first time, Chevrolet wanted its car in Europe, and the name had to be easily translatable. ZR1, the small-block racing package intro-duced in 1970, fit nicely.

Following the media introductions through Switzer-land and France, Lloyd Reuss and his colleagues had another production reality to face. They had built only 84 preproduction prototypes for engineering, media preview, and photography with 1989 VINs. Chevrolet sold none of them, and on April 19, 1989, it notified dealers that the ZR1 option would not be available until model year 1990.

U.S. buyers had to take normal-production Corvettes for 1989, with their six-speed transmission and FX3 adjustable suspension. This was no slouch, to be sure, but by midway through the model year, the enthusiast magazines were characterizing the anticipated ZR1 as the second coming.

The production ZR1 was finally introduced for the 1990 model year. The option cost $27,016 on top of the base price of the $31,979 coupe. Some 3,049 buyers couldn't resist and paid $58,995 for the car. Though pricier than previous Corvettes, it was still one-third the price of Ferrari's Tes-tarossa and 20 percent less than the Porsche 928GT. And the ZR1 beat both those cars to 60 miles per hour by 1.5 sec-onds. Due to gas-guzzler burdens, CAFE requirements, and EPA mandates, Chevrolet rated the LT5 at 375 horsepower.

Design redid the interior for 1990, replacing the instrument panel with a new console (now a combina-tion of LCDs, light shows, and analog dials), door pan-els, and driver's-side airbag. They gave buyers a real,

working glove compartment, replacing the long-lived but unloved breadloaf.

Chevrolet engineers created a "valet switch" protection for ZR1 owners. The owner twisted a key to override the ECM so that no matter what throttle position the parking attendant (or teenage offspring) might try, only the milder injection tube operated.

Production in 1990 amounted to 16,016 coupes, including 3,049 ZR1s, and 7,630 convertibles, for a total of 23,646 cars. Production in 1991 decreased to 14,967 coupes, and convertible sales also slipped, to 5,672. Among the coupes, 2,044 were ZR1s, for which Chevrolet increased the price by a substantial $4,676 to $31,683, or a grand total of $64,138 for the second-edition of the lim-ited-production coupes.

Chevrolet made what many thought was a mistake in 1991. They adopted for all models the squared taillights first introduced on the 1990 production ZR1s. While the hotter car still wore wider bodywork, 1990 owners had expressed pleasure when others recognized the subtle dis-tinction; 1991 buyers made their discontent known when that uniqueness was taken away.

1992: A Year of Change

Model year 1992 brought numerous changes, including a new LT1 small-block power plant, an electronic traction control to more successfully get power to the ground and keep it there, and a new Goodyear tire to further aid that task. When the new LT1 reached showrooms 20 years after the original 370-horsepower LT1 disappeared in 1972, it produced 300 net horsepower and provided a 0–60 miles per hour times of four seconds, three full seconds faster than the 1972 model. While the old LT1 consumed 12 miles per gallon, the new engine, with 50 horsepower more than the L98, returned 17 miles per gallon city and 25 highway.

The Bosch Acceleration Slip Regulation (ASR) performed like its ABS (antilock braking system) in reverse, controlling wheel spin under acceleration. The ASR worked liked an instantaneously reactive, very intelligent, limited-slip differential. With the ASR coupled with Goodyear's new Eagle directional, asymmetrical GS-C P275/40Z–17 tires front and rear, Formula One and Indy race-car technology for wet and damp and dry racing came to the street.

On July 2, 1992, many of the principals who were responsible for making the Corvette what it had become gathered in Bowling Green for a celebration. The one millionth car, a white convertible, drove off the line. It went just a few blocks into storage, where it would await completion of its new home about a quarter-mile from the end of the Bowling Green assembly line.

Board members of the National Corvette Restorers Society voted in November 1988 to establish a national Corvette museum. Setting a budget of $6 million, they raised funds, acquired a site, and selected building architects and exhibit designers. They opened the 68,000-square-foot structure, constructed alongside Interstate

It became a costly package. The base coupe started at $34,595. Adding the ZR1 alone boosted the price another $31,683. Chevrolet produced only 448 ZR-1s, and no one complained about the extra 30 horsepower.

65, in 1994. Now they routinely display as many as 80 Corvettes at a time. The ever-changing exhibits usually include equal numbers of cars on loan from GM's own collection and from private collectors around the world, as well as cars owned by the nonprofit museum courtesy of generous donations. Following its opening, the National Corvette Museum quickly became a mecca for Corvette enthusiasts.

The Quest for More Power

The big news for 1993 was that Midgley's and McLellan's goal of 400-plus horsepower under the hood of the ZR1 made its way to the dealerships. Engineering subtly changed intake valve head shape and the valve seat to improve fuel flow and overall breathing. This micro-tinkering brought output to 405 horsepower. Goodyear's asymmetrical GS-C's improved wet-weather maneuverability over the Gatorbacks at the modest cost of dry-pavement acceleration. Zero-to-sixty miles per hour times slipped from 4.2 to 4.5 seconds.

Outside and inside the car, Chevrolet celebrated the Corvette's 40th anniversary with the Z25 appearance option, available for $1,455, providing Ruby Red exterior paint and interior leather. Some 6,749 were produced. Total production of the 1993 car crept up slightly to 21,590, with 5,692 convertibles (at $41,195 base) and 15,898 coupes (at $34,595). Only 448 were ZR1 options, still at $31,683 extra, despite the new engine.

Chevrolet upgraded the PASS-key system introduced in 1986 with the addition of the new Passive Keyless Entry

The 40th Anniversary package provided Ruby Red leather sport seats; the driver's was power adjusted. All leather seats sold for model year 1993 had a 40th Anniverary logo stitched in, whether or not the commemorative package was ordered.

(PKE). Engineering imbedded a tiny transmitter in the key fob that signaled one of two receivers in the car body to open one or both doors and light the interior. As owners walked away with their keys in pocket or purse, the PKE automatically locked their car and set the alarm, confirmed by a brief toot of the horn. If the key fob is still in the car when the driver walks away, nothing happens. No horn sounding was a reminder to return for the keys.

Corvette engineers replaced the recently reintroduced glove compartment with a passenger-side airbag in 1994, and this provided the opportunity for an interior makeover. The interior studio redesigned the seats, making them more comfortable to a wider variety of bodies.

Goodyear introduced Extended Mobility Tires (EMTs), essentially run-flat rubber useful at zero air pressure for up to 200 miles at speeds as fast as 55 miles per hour. A monitor on the instrument panel alerted the driver of low—or no—pressure. Corvettes still carried spare tires, jacks, and tire irons, and the EMT option was available only on about 5,000 of the 1994 model-year cars with

either the FX3 option (with slightly softer springs) or the base suspension, but not the Z01 or ZR1.

Engineering and electronics engineers replaced the Engine Control Module (ECM) with a new powertrain control module (PCM) to govern the transmission and also the new sequential-port fuel injection. In this system, the injectors worked simultaneously with the engine-firing order, offering smoother idle, quicker throttle response, and reduced exhaust emissions.

Production numbers for 1994 inched up again. Total Bowling Green output was 23,330 cars, of which 17,984 were coupes and 5,346 convertibles. Chevrolet sold only 448 ZR1s, though the price dropped a few dollars to $67,443, as more equipment was made standard on the base car. The bleed-through of engineering from the ZR1 to the LT1 had produced a car so good that with few options (the G92 performance axle at only $50 and the FX3 electronic ride and handling option at $1,695), a buyer came very close to a ZR1. The ZR1's supplemental 105 horsepower made the biggest difference in speed ranges few owners ever saw, and insurance companies began to react to the ZR1 code as they had to muscle cars in the late 1960s and early 1970s.

The Indianapolis Motor Speedway chose the 1995 Corvette as the 500-mile pace car. Palmer's designers developed a wild dark purple and white scheme, and Chevrolet offered replicas to the public. They sold only 527; the two-tone combination put off more people than it attracted. In total, 4,971 convertibles sold, and Chevrolet repeated 1994 ZR1 production with just 448 cars, with total coupe sales for 1995 amounting to 15,771.

In anticipation of the C5 introduction, previously scheduled for 1996, Chevrolet discontinued the ZR1 package at the end of production of 1995 cars. Even when management acknowledged that the C5 would not be available until 1997, they let the ZR1 disappear. Mercury Marine assembled the last LT5 engine in November 1993. The total ZR1 count was 6,939 from 1990 through 1995.

Farewell, C4

Spy photos confirmed that the C5 was coming and that 1996 was the final year for C4. Once again, customers wrestled with waiting for the unknown new car or buying the familiar. To give them something to consider, Chevrolet released its new 330-horsepower LT4. Engineering used a new aluminum-head design, new camshaft, and Crane roller-bearing rocker arms.

Externally, designers and product planners created two packages with visual appeal. The first was a silver-painted Collector Edition, the Z15, for $1,250. Besides color and special trim, it used ZR1 wheels (but not the tires), also painted silver. More exciting visually was the Grand Sport Package Z16. Chevrolet produced only 1,000 of these in coupe or convertible form ($2,880 for the convertible option, $3,250 for the coupe). Coupes used the full ZR1 wheel and tire option, including the fat, squat P315/35ZR-17 rears, barely contained by fender flares (not body panels, like the ZR1). Convertible Grand Sports took advantage of the tire package for the Collector Edition. Chevrolet painted the cars Admiral Blue with twin white racing stripes centered on the car and bright red hashes across the left front fender.

Chevrolet replaced the previous FX3 suspension with F45, "Selective Real Time Damping," a new active system that took road surface and suspension load inputs 60 times per second, revising shock characteristics with equal frequency. Chevrolet produced 21,536 1996 models, including the Grand Sports and 5,412 Collector Editions. The new $1,695 LT4 engine option went into nearly a third of the cars.

Chevrolet carried on its fourth-edition Corvette for 13 years, another long run for a popular car. It sold 368,180 over that span, earning GM nearly $100 million in profits. The car withstood attacks by Nissan's 300ZX, Acura's NSX, Mitsubishi's 3000GT VR-4, Porsche's 959, 944, and 968, and Dodge's 10-cylinder Viper. Lamborghini replaced its Countach with the Diablo, which for all its bravado represented only a slight movement of the benchmark. Only Ferrari, with its race-car-like F40 and F50, and England's Gordon Murray, with his $1 million McLaren three-seat F1, moved into such rarified space that few could approach. Corvette's competitors came and went. They kept on coming, and to their chagrin, so did Corvette.

THE C5 ARRIVES

CHAPTER TEN

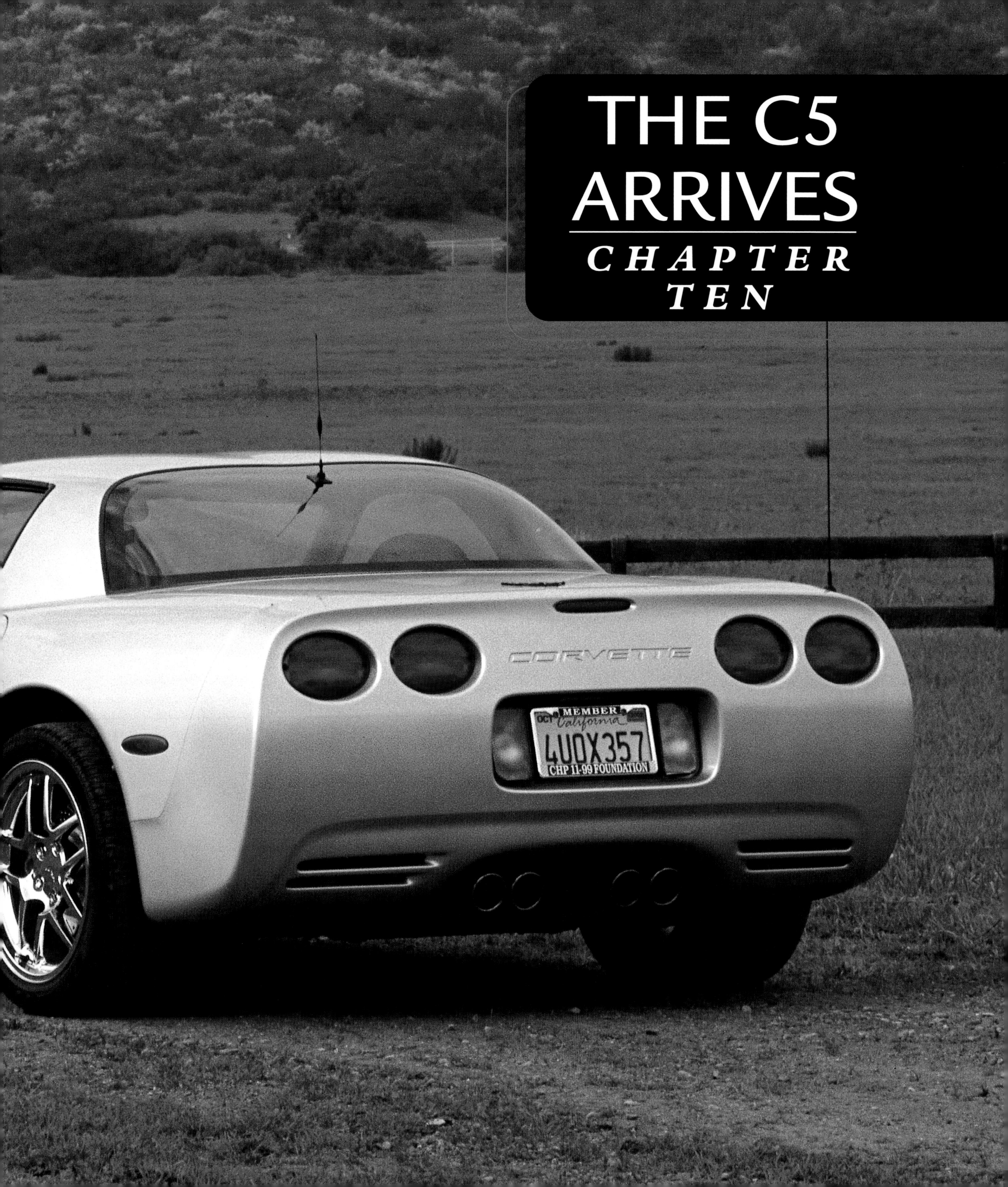

chapter ten

THE C5
ARRIVES

1997–2003

The C5 first emerged in the imaginations of a few dedicated individuals as early as August 1988, with intentions of introducing it for the 1993 model year. Between then and its eventual introduction as a 1997 car, the next-generation C5 Corvette endured a Shakespearean saga. The C5 came into being despite diligent efforts by antagonists determined to make new rules, challenge and obstruct the car-building process, and stop this car at every chance they could.

Author James Schefter recorded the dramas that yielded the C5 in his book, *All Corvettes Are Red*. Its title comes from a quote from John Heinricy, Corvette racer, endurance record holder, and supervisor of the C4 until the end of the program. Heinricy maintains that all other colors are just mistakes. Schefter's history takes readers deep inside GM to explain how the C5 came to be.

Titanic egos played roles in this story. Titanic describes their size and, in a few cases, their end. During the car's eight-year gestation—coinciding with the darkest days of the automobile industry's economy—thousands of employees left the industry. GM lost hundreds of

Previous pages and opposite: *(previous spread) Among the Z06's unique cosmetic touches are the black air scoops for the rear brakes and the split-spoke wheels with a chrome finish. The C5's reversed air scoop behind the front wheel echoes Corvette designs of the past, while the car's aerodynamic shape pushes the modern wedge silhouette of recent Corvettes even further into the future.*

Corvette again paced the Indy 500 but this time the color scheme was harder for many people to take. Wild graphics adorned a Pace Car Purple finish. The package included bright yellow-painted wheels though these magnesium wheels were a popular option. Chevrolet produced 1,163 replicas (for an extra $5,039) and most owners quickly removed the gaudy exterior graphics decals.

employees, including key engineers. So many engineers had left that barely enough remained to do the work during some critical junctures in the C5's development. Ford's and Chrysler's engineering departments took their pick from among hundreds of experienced, qualified individuals who left GM because of worries that the company might go bankrupt. As Chevrolet reinvented its Corvette, General Motors, which had reorganized before C5 development started, would reorganize itself a second and third time.

To the outside world, GM's profit statements looked healthy. Inside, the picture was bleak and drawn in red ink. Cost containment realities slipped the 1993 launch back to 1994, and by midyear more bad financial news forced the C5 back to 1995.

A Six-Year Car

Each reschedule led to new design directives. Chuck Jordan, GM's vice president of design since 1986, delivered the messages to his increasingly impatient designers. Jordan rewarded John Cafaro, who had created the C4's basic shape and its signature clamshell hood, with primary design authority for the C5. As each quarter's financial statements brought another year's delay to introduction,

CHAPTER TEN

Jordan stressed to anyone who would listen that the Japanese were not standing still and could bring their cars out in three years. The Japanese were the Corvette's target competition, and the C5 was on the way to being a six-year car.

GM's bean counters voiced their own perspective. Unlike any other GM product, this division sold every Corvette it produced. In 1989, the U.S. government had ended the car-loan interest deduction. Every U.S.-built model lost sales, except Corvette. It continued to bring in profits, something like $4,000 per car, each year after the initial investment was paid off. Production was paid for at 16,500 cars; in 1989, Chevy sold 16,663 coupes, meaning the 163 coupes and all 9,749 convertibles made profits, nearly $40 million worth. Still, when GM's management got a clear view of its financial picture in late fall, it appeared that the Chevrolet-Pontiac-Canada (CPC) group, home of the Corvette, might lose $2.6 billion in 1990. At that point, the new Corvette was derailed indefinitely.

Bean counters could demonstrate that expensive engineering, such as the 1990s ZR1 program, had not proven financially beneficial to Chevrolet. But the C4 chassis was a problem that needed engineering attention. The decision was made to totally re-engineer the car's frame.

Thin-walled steel produced under high pressure provided the strength of the old frame with much less weight. Using a technique called hydroforming, engineering formed the major frame rails for the C5, one on each side, from a single piece of rolled, welded steel. The new rails started out as 14-foot-long sheets 2 millimeters thick. The new process rolled these into a 6-inch-diameter tube and then laser welded them shut. The tubes went into a 200-ton press that filled them with water at 7,000-psi pressure. The water pressure expanded the tube like a sausage. The press shaped and bent the steel into the bends and rectangular channels inside the mold. They came out of the press at a rate of 15 an hour, 13 feet long and perfect.

GM allocated $250 million for development of the C5. While this was a sizable sum, it left little allowance for false starts or missteps, and it forced engineering and design to

This was the third body incarnation that Chevrolet General Manager Jim Perkins conceived when he approved the C5 project. With its fixed hardtop welded in place, it weighed 80 pounds less than the coupe and was 12 percent stiffer.

work side-by-side to meet their goal. The two sides created a car with nearly five times as much resistance to twisting and flexing as the C4—another benefit of this collaborative working arrangement and the hydroformed chassis. This backbone chassis encouraged them to use a transaxle, a one-piece transmission-differential bolted directly to the rear axle. Moving this weight rearward allowed for a nearly 50/50 front-to-rear weight balance. With the transmission bulk out of the cockpit foot well, designers and engineers moved the entire compartment forward slightly, opening up rear space for a luggage compartment. Golf was the game of business. Japanese cars accommodated two golf bags. Now so did the Corvette.

In summer 1990, GM's board named Bob Stempel, a former engineer and former general manager of Chevrolet, as its chairman, and Lloyd Reuss became president. Though they were longtime Corvette supporters, they had a corporation to save. GM was in deep trouble and the Corvette took another big hit.

James Schefter reported that, instead of a C5 for 1995, the board ordered a thorough re-skin for the C4, slipping the C5 back to 1998. All passenger cars sold in the United States for 1997 had to have side-impact protection, however, which required a structure that engineering could not retrofit into the C4. Recognizing this, Reuss reinstated the C5 budget, to cover a new body, new backbone chassis, and a 1996 launch. The C5 would be introduced first as a Targa-roof coupe. A full convertible would appear for 1997, as well as an entry-level hardtop, a $25,000 to $30,000 concept close to Perkins' heart, a boy-racer he nicknamed "Billy Bob."

Then the corporation's profit and loss statements arrived. CPC lost $3.3 billion, not the $2.6 predicted. Projections hinted that GM could be bankrupt sometime in

1997–2003 1997–2003 1997–2003 1997–2003 1997–2003 1997–2003 1997–2003 1997–2003 1997–2003

1991. The board cut Corvette's budget, and the car slipped to 1997. GM lost $4.5 billion in 1991. Lloyd Reuss was relieved of his duties. Bob Stempel resigned in October 1992, and John Smale replaced Stempel as board chairman. Dave McLellan and Chuck Jordan followed Stempel and Reuss out the door, both retiring the following year. The board warned engineering to find a way to retrofit side-impact protection to the C4 as a worst-case scenario for 1997.

According to Schefter, the first drivable C5 test vehicle was a $1.2 million mule called CERV-4. Soon after, there was a half-price copy, the CERV-4b. Engineering set 1993 C4 bodies on C5 frames and ran them around Milford and GM's Desert Proving Ground in Mesa, Arizona. They were indistinguishable except that they had a trunk. There was scarcely any money available from the board to create these most necessary first cars, so Jim Perkins discretely funneled other division funds into the Corvette program he'd fought so hard to preserve.

After the CERVs came "alpha" and then "beta" test cars, each wearing close-to-correct C5 bodies that were heavily disguised. Engineering assembled these two, closely matching production specifications. Then came prototypes, nearly perfect from an engineering and design point of view, fabricated from preproduction versions of production parts. As testers devoured the prototypes, prepilot cars began to appear, the first ones assembled in Bowling Green starting in August 1996. "Pilot" cars, the first saleable production vehicles, were initiated a month later. By this time, John Middlebrook had taken over Chevrolet command from Perkins, who had retired feeling fairly certain that the C5 would appear.

The two CERVs used C4 engines and existed primarily to examine the chassis. Interiors were cobbled together to test heating, ventilation, and air-conditioning. Engineering created a new power plant for the C5, known as Gen III. It was an all-new third-generation version of the decades-old Chevy small block. Responses from thousands of owner and customer surveys reinforced another ZR1 lesson. Corvette owners wanted torque, not turbos or superchargers. They didn't want the added expense of four-valve heads with dual-overhead camshafts. Dave Hill, Dave McLellan's replacement, knew pushrod engines were not as tall as overhead-cam and multivalve engines. Keeping the low hood also improved forward visibility and was essential to achieve the aerodynamic drag-coefficient targets that were crucial to meeting fuel-consumption goals.

Engineering cast the Gen III engine in aluminum to save weight. The aim was to get the car below 3,500 pounds with full tanks, two passengers, and luggage. Every pound of weight increased fuel consumption and tire, brake, and engine wear. Excess weight decreased shock-absorber life, added strain to chassis and driveline, and detracted from performance. Research figures showed that improved acceleration time equated with increased sales. Weight became an obsession.

John Cafaro's sleek body had gotten aerodynamic adjustments from engineer Kurt Romberg, who shaved its shape. The C5 measured 0.293-ci displacement in the wind tunnel, the lowest of any production vehicle made anywhere except for GM's EV1 electric vehicle. With twin gas tanks straddling the rear axle and new Goodyear run-flat extended-mobility tires requiring no spare, the C5 offered 23.8 cubic feet of trunk space, more than Cadillac's largest full-size sedans. Engineering found ways to eliminate more than 1,400 separate parts from the previous car, each piece costing from fractions of a cent to many dollars. Eliminating these parts also cut 69 pounds from the 1996 C4 weight. The body, formed in plastic rather than fiberglass, saved weight as well. The C5 used sheet-molded compound-plastic (SMC) and reaction injection-molded plastic (RIM). These technologies produced lighter, stronger, and more rigid panels.

The rear suspension no longer relied on the half-axles to perform suspension duties. Upper control arms locked the rear wheels into place much more accurately. As a byproduct of the C5's stiffer backbone frame, engineers softened the transverse fiberglass springs technology adapted from the C4. This allowed a better ride and kept the tires in contact even with surface changes in the road.

The Gen III LS1 engine produced 345 horsepower, 15 more than the C4's LT4. This moved the car from 0 to 60 miles per hour in 4.7 seconds with the six-speed manual gearbox. EPA fuel economy numbers were published as 18 city/29 highway miles per gallon. Chevy quoted top speed at 172 miles per hour.

While magazine reviewers loved the car, buyers barely sauntered to dealerships. With only a fastback coupe available, Chevrolet produced just 9,752 of them at a base price of $37,495. But the pace accelerated throughout the 1998 model year when Jim Perkins' convertible appeared. It weighed 114 pounds less than the 1996 convertible and was four times stiffer. Though its trunk, the first in a Corvette convertible since 1962, measured just 13.8 cubic feet, it still held two full golf bags. It sold for $44,425.

After interviewing other "tuners," the owners went to Chuck Mallett of Berea, Ohio, looking for a 50-state legal, street-drivable car that could run 200 miles per hour in order to win a Nevada open road race. Only Mallett could deliver a car that could also pass California's stringent smog tests.

CHAPTER TEN

Mallett's options include lowering the car 1.5 inches, fitting Fikse three-piece forged alloy wheels, and a catalog full of other things. Basic conversion to the Mallett 435 cost $34,650, though nothing about the result is basic.

Chevrolet produced 11,849 convertibles and 19,235 coupes. Of the 31,084 Corvettes manufactured, 5,356 featured the optional active-handling system, a $500 version of the earlier racing GTP's immensely complicated suspension. Fewer buyers selected the $5,408 Indy Pace Car replica option. Its vivid purple exterior, wild graphics, yellow wheels, and yellow and black leather interior spoke to only 1,163 souls.

Production numbers for 1999 road-going cars were strong, with a total of 33,270 produced, including 4,031 of the new hardtop that Perkins first envisioned. His plan was to provide privateer racers an "option deleted" fixed-roof version, with cloth seats, no air-conditioning, power steering, brakes, windows, door locks, no radio, and rubber mats in place of interior carpeting. Weekend hobbyists could trailer these to parking lot Auto Cross or SCCA Solo I events. When accountants examined Perkins' first proposal, they revised the description, because losing the profitable options would cost the division too much. So the hardtop arrived well equipped.

The 1998 Corvette model was named the North American Car of the Year by the automotive media during the North American International Auto Show in Detroit.

That's not low altitude flight velocity. That's all four wheels on the ground during the Silver State 100, an unlimited speed open road race over Nevada highways. This car won the 2001 event by 2 seconds.

Going to the Track

On November 4, 1998, Chevrolet general manager John Middlebrook made a startling announcement. Chevrolet was going sports car racing—and not in some clandestine Zora Arkus-Duntov manner in which various engineers coincidentally took vacations during race weekends at Daytona, Sebring, or Le Mans. This was a full-on and very public effort. The program would be overseen by GM's motorsports manager, Herb Fischel, and its racing program manager, Doug Fehan. They intended to compete internationally in FIA's category GT2. To meet that category's requirements, the racer

car's chassis had to be production-based, the engines production-derived, and bodies only slightly modified. The Corvette would race head-to-head against twin-turbo Porsche 911 GTs and V-10 Vipers, among others. The C5-R would debut at the 24 Hours of Daytona on January 30 and 31, 1999, then move on to the Sebring 12 Hours and through several of the Petit Le Mans series events in preparation to attempt the full 24-hour French race in June 2000.

Fischel and Fehan tagged Ken Brown, the engineer who had designed the C5's chassis and suspension, to design the C5-R. Corvette brand manager Jim Campbell told them that their "primary focus was to improve the breed," and "to squeeze valuable engineering information from each lap Corvette turns on the racetrack." They reduced the weight to 2,510 pounds, a decrease of 735 pounds from the production car. Reproducing the production body in carbon fiber helped save weight. It needed only minor attention from aerodynamicist Brian Miller, who developed front underbody ducting to assist with engine cooling, downforce, and drag. He also added a rear wing and rear diffusers. FIA rules strictly prescribed horsepower output based on vehicle weight, which increased the technical challenges. To meet the formula, Joe Negri, GM's motorsports engine director, revised engine dimensions from the production Gen III LS1's 346-ci displacement to 365-ci displacement. Chevrolet published output as 600 horsepower at 7,200 rpm. By the end of the 24-hour Daytona race, drivers Ron Fellows, John Paul Jr., and Chris Kniefel had nursed their silver and black C5-R #2 through a time-consuming and position-sacrificing morning oil leak to finish 3rd in GT2 and 18th overall, having climbed as high as 5th overall through much of the night. The second car, #4, finished well back after breaking a rear suspension upright. While everyone had hoped for better results, racing is an alchemist's blend of preparation and luck. By season's end, Fehan and his crew had learned valuable lessons about parts and tracks. They committed to run at least four events in 2000.

Corvette Enters the New Millennium

Model year 2000 was one of refinements, improvements, revisions, increases, and continuing healthy sales. Hard-top production dipped almost in half to 2,090, but overall figures totaled 33,682, and Corvette's racing effort officially reached Le Mans. Following a February second-place overall finish behind a French-entered Viper GTS-R, Chevrolet prepared to go abroad. Plans were already floating to promote and sell the C5 in Europe and Great Britain. European journalists told *Corvette Quarterly* editor John Stein that they considered the Corvette more a touring car than a sports car. That was before the race. When the race ended on June 18, the #63 Corvette, having had its racing transmission replaced in 16 minutes, set the quickest laps in GTS class, ahead of every Porsche and faster than the Vipers. With two hours to go, the #64 car lost its starter in the pits, consuming another 12 minutes for replacement. Then the checkered flag fell. Corvettes finished 10th and 11th overall, 3rd and 4th in GTS class. Dave Hill told John Stein that he was "very glad we came."

The following year, Ron Fellows, Chris Kniefel, Frank Freon, and Johnny O'Connell brought their C5-R home in first place—first overall and first in class—at Daytona International Speedway on February 1, 2001. The two Corvettes were split by a pair of GT1 Porsches, identical to models that had won Le Mans in 1998. Fellows' car averaged 97.3 miles per hour over 2,335.4 miles. Just four-and-a-half months later, Corvettes proved that Daytona was no fluke, finishing first and second in GTS class at the 24 Hours of Le Mans and establishing the car's reputation worldwide.

For the production cars, Chevrolet resurrected the Z06 racing-model designation in the fall of 2000, which

The original LS6 Z06 option provided buyers with 385 horsepower. Several internal modifications brought that output up to 405 horsepower for this 2002 model. The original Z06 was a racer's package available in 1963.

brought wide grins and wild eyes even to Corvette buyers who just wanted to grand tour. Available only in the hardtop body, the 2001 model car reminded historians and racers alike of the ZR1 models from 1990 and even Arkus-Duntov's first production racers from 1963. With 385 horsepower in a 3,115-pound car, the Z06 achieved 0–60 miles per hour in 4.0 seconds flat, half a second quicker than the ZR1s. The car's interior was slightly less refined than the convertibles' or coupes', but its nature was performance at the expense of grand touring. Stronger valve springs allowed its LS6 engine to reach 6,500 rpm where the standard LS1 was limited to 6,000 rpm. Design and engineering fitted red engine covers under the hood, and red-disc brake calipers peeked through the wheels. The Z06 arrived as Corvette's highest priced variant, at $47,500, just $500 more than the convertible. Production finished at 5,773 copies for its first year.

> ## Chevrolet designers and engineers in Detroit and assemblers in Bowling Green did such a good job refining the 2002 car that J.D. Power named it the best premium sports car in their Initial Quality Study.

For model year 2002, Chevrolet continued to improve its production Corvettes. It boosted Z06 output to a muscle car–era 405 horsepower by fitting slightly softer piston rings, using a well-known NASCAR engine-builder's trick that allows even higher engine speeds.

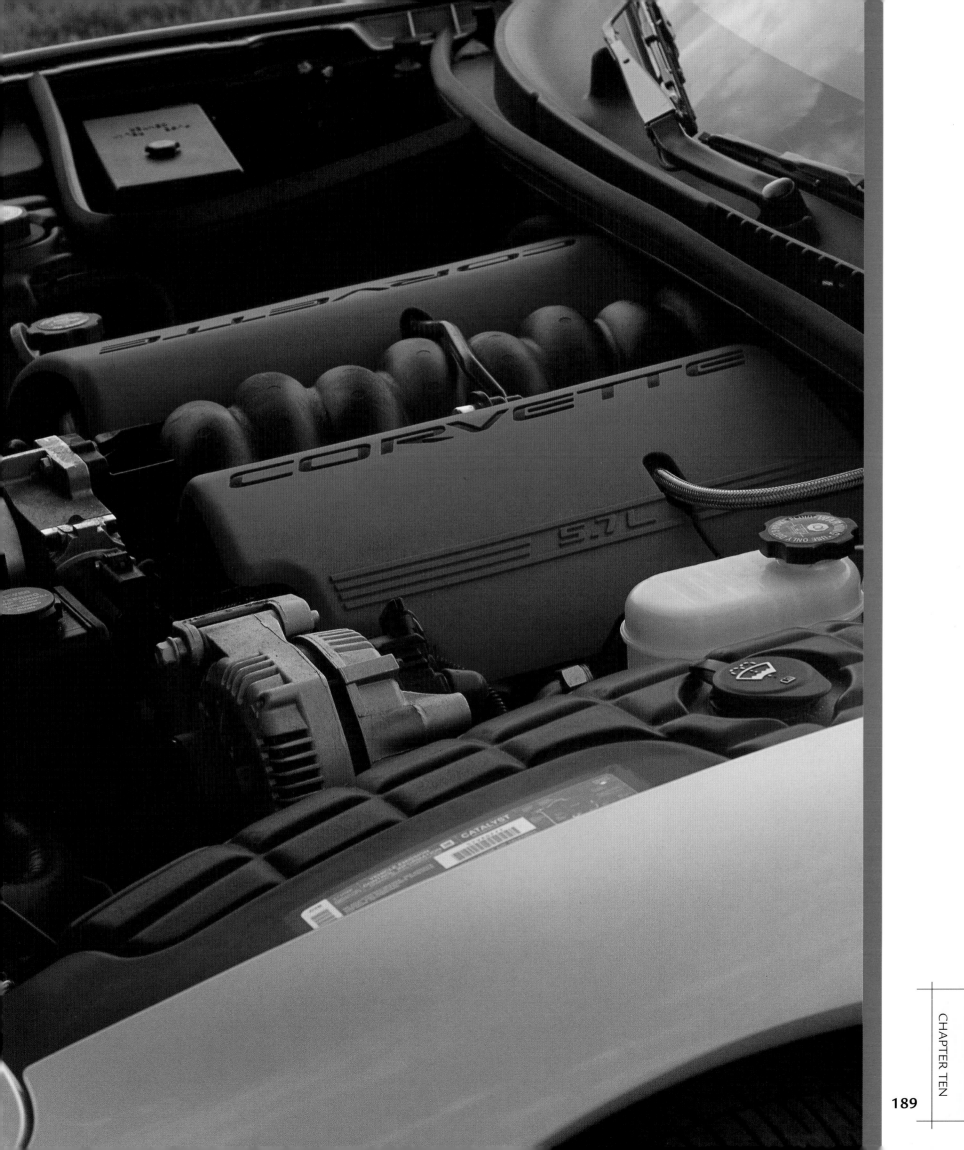

Only the hardtop body was stiff enough to handle the potential of the new LS6 engine and Z06 package. Both numbers harkened back to higher performance times (the LS6 was Chevrolet's monstrous 454-ci muscle engine in the early 1970s.)

The future and time wait for no one. In a Pasadena design studio, clay modelers fashion concepts of the C6. Conceived at one time to be the 50th anniversary model, it has been slipped back like many before it. Those who have been privileged to see the shapes have struggled for words, and then finally concluded that "if they build that one, they'll blow everybody else off the road. Everybody!"

The visual lineage of the car has evolved more subtly through the C4 into the C5, whereas changes from the C1 through the C2 to the C3 were more radical. But these design and engineering decisions are based on money and courage and faith and optimism. The Europeans say that winning at Le Mans is not a one-time thing, but racing is staggeringly expensive and no corporation will continue when money gets tight or priorities change or other products need massive infusions. Yet the Corvette has made money and it has made converts. The C4 brought us the ZR1 and world distance records. The C5 brought us the Z06 and world-class, headline-making racing victories. It is tantalizing to slip into a new Corvette, squint past the heads-up information display, and try to imagine the road ahead for America's favorite sports car.

Index